COLLINS GEM

HILLWALKER'S
Survival Guide

Barry Davies

HarperCollins*Publishers*

Barry Davies is an ex-member of the SAS and is also the author of *Collins Gem SAS Self-Defence*

HarperCollins Publishers
PO Box, Glasgow G4 0NB

First published 1999

Reprint 10 9 8 7 6 5 4 3 2 1

© Barry Davies, 1999

ISBN 0 00 472203-5

US Distributor:
Lewis International Inc.
2201 NW 102 Place # 1
Miami
FL 33172
USA
(Tel. 800 259 5962 / 305 436 7984
Fax. 800 664 5095 / 305 436 7985)

Printed in Italy by Amadeus S.p.A.

Contents

Introduction	**6**

Chapter One – Planning	**7**
Preparation	7
Walking and Walk-leading	11
Contacts for Advice on Walking	17

Chapter Two – Rights of Way	**18**
England and Wales	19
Scotland	20
Types of Rights of Way	21
What Your Rights Allow	22
Responsibilites for Rights of Way	22
Open Country Access Land	24
Common Land	24
Forestry Commission	25
National Trusts	25
Common Problems and Obstructions	25
Conservation	43

Chapter Three – Clothing and Equipment	**44**
Overheating and Sweating	45
How the Layer System Works	45
Head, Hands and Feet	47
Keeping Clothing in Good Repair	48
Survival Clothing	50
Boots and Footwear	51
Rucksacks	54

Chapter Four – Navigation	**60**
Ordnance Survey Maps	61
Compass	62
Orientating a Map	64
Finding a Grid Reference	64

Magnetic Variation   66
Taking a Compass Bearing from the Map   68
Keeping on Course   69
Putting a Compass Bearing on the Map   70
GPS (Global Positioning System)   71
Finding Direction without a Compass   72
Obstacles   76
How to Move in the Dark   80

Chapter Five – Camping Out   85

Barns and Bothies   85
Camp Sites   86
Choosing a Tent   87
Emergency Shelters   90
Forms of Quick Shelter   93
Sleeping Bags   96
Survival Bags and Insulation Mats   98
Cookers   99
Fire-lighting   103
Heat-sources   108

Chapter Six – Food   112

Chapter Seven – Water   118

Chapter Eight – Medical   123

First-aid Kit   124
Breathing Means Life   126
Artificial Respiration   130
Medical Emergencies   134
Bleeding   135
Shock   140
Fractures   141
Carrying an Injured Person   143

Concussion and Skull Fractures 145
Burns 145
Heat Exhaustion 147
Keeping Warm 148
Hypothermia 150
Cramp 153
Blisters 154
Hygiene and Sanitation 155
Precautions Against Things that Bite 156
Snakes 160
Bears 160
Poisonous Plants 161

Chapter Nine – The Weather 162

Weather Forecasts 164

Chapter Ten – Winter Hillwalking 166

Fitness 166
Precautions 167
Avalanches 167
Using an Ice Axe 169

Chapter Eleven – Search and Rescue 172

Injury 172
Lost 173
Fear 174
Shelter and Survival 175
Survival Kit 176
Going for Help 178
Alone 179
Mountain Rescue Teams 181
Signalling 185
When Help Arrives 190

Chapter Twelve – Useful Addresses 191

Introduction

At some time or another we have all relished the pleasures of walking through the hills and countryside of the British Isles. However, walking in mountainous terrain brings with it potential problems, so in order to avoid these as much as possible and to enjoy fully this wonderful pastime, *Gem Hillwalker's Survival Guide* has been specifically designed as a handy-sized *aide-mémoire* to the hillwalking experience. While it is comprehensive it does not labour any one subject or seek to be a pure survival book; if anything, it can be described as a logical guide detailing how to prepare for a walk and what to do should the unexpected happen.

This is my third survival book; when writing I draw on a wealth of experience, mainly from my eighteen years with the SAS as a member of Mountain Troop. During this time I spent two years as an SAS survival instructor at the International Long Range Patrol School (ILRPS) in southern Germany. This involved teaching survival to fast jet pilots and special forces who attended the school from all over the world. Many of the courses were conducted in the Bavarian countryside, where hillwalking became part of the daily routine.

On leaving the SAS I became involved with BCB International Ltd, the world's largest producer of outdoor survival products. In addition to my service with the SAS and association with BCB International Ltd, I have also gained from personally exploring the superb landscape of the British Isles.

The *Hillwalker's Survival Guide* provides up-to-date information on preparation, countryside law, navigation, weather, medical emergencies and rescue. It uses a clear format to guide the walker through problems that can and often do arise. No matter where you walk, *Gem Hillwalker's Survival Guide* will prove an essential part of your equipment, indispensable for its knowledge and information.

Planning

Any hillwalking journey, whether a several-day camping
trip or just a short walk, should be planned carefully.
Diligent preparation is essential to ensure that the trip is
both pleasant and successful. Certain guidelines,
although seeming over-fussy and restrictive, could well
save a life if followed correctly. Guidelines are even more
vital when a group of young or inexperienced people
takes to the hills with little or no knowledge of map-
reading or survival skills. In such a case it is up to the
party leader to be responsible for the implementation of
and strict adherence to certain safety procedures, albeit
without losing the excitement of the outing.

PREPARATION

Once the location has been decided on, as much
information as possible about the area needs to be
gathered. Maps, guidebooks and local people can all
provide valuable facts on good, interesting routes. In
particular, make sure that the location is accessible at the
time you are planning to go, and that, if the land is
private, you have permission from the landowner to walk
across it. If you are planning a walking holiday it is best
to ask permission this well in advance to avoid any
disappointment. If the trip is to last more than a day,
plan each day so that places of interest and targets can be
reached in relative comfort.

Another aspect to consider is how you are going to get to
the starting point. If using public transport, how close

will you be able to get to the start of your planned walking route and is there public transport at the other end? If you intend using private transport, remember to park carefully where you will not cause a nuisance or an obstruction (such as in a farm gateway), and preferably use a designated car park. Vehicles should not be taken on private roads or bridleways, or driven more than 15 m (45 ft) from a highway without the landowner's permission.

Taking into account the duration of your walk, you should consider appropriate clothing, footwear and essential equipment. If you are in a group, it is important that the group leader checks that each individual is properly prepared prior to setting off.

Check that you have parked your vehicle with care – do not block or restrict any access

Essential Hillwalking Equipment Checklist

- Map and compass (see page 60)
- Boots and socks (see page 51)
- Rucksack (see page 55)
- Waterproof clothing (see page 46)
- Spare clothing
- Hat and gloves
- First-aid kit (see page 124)
- Survival kit (see page 176)
- Sun barrier cream
- Means of starting a fire (see page 103)
- Water canteens (full)
- Means of water purification (see page 121)
- Small stove
- Small cooking pot
- Mug and plate/Mess kit
- Food
- Knife
- Torch and spare batteries
- Walking pole (depending on the terrain and the individual)
- For winter walking, extra equipment is required (see page 166)

Essential Camping Out Equipment Checklist

- Tent (see page 87)
- Sleeping bag (see page 96)
- Insulation mat (see page 98)
- Inflatable pillow
- Large water carrier
- Lantern
- Notebook/pencil
- Camera/binoculars
- Camp shoes
- Toiletries
- Toilet paper
- Insect repellent

Before setting off on your walk, check the following points:

- Check that you have an appropriate map as well as a compass, and that you know how to use them.
- Explain to the **whole** group where you are going and point out safety routes in the event of an emergency.
- Check the contents of your rucksack, placing all items such as spare clothing and sleeping bags in a waterproof plastic bag. Make sure your rucksack is comfortable.
- Check your clothing to ensure that you are wearing or carrying sufficient layers to cope with any weather changes. Wear purpose-made walking boots, with a

decent tread and upper support. Doc Martens and trainers will land you in trouble. Your boots should be broken in and comfortable. Check you have plasters in your medical kit, just in case.

- It is essential that you have full waterproof clothing. If this is not worn it should be placed near the top of your rucksack.
- Carry enough food and water for the party, evenly distributed. Choose carbohydrate- and energy-rich food, e.g. chocolate or Kendal Mint Cake, and drinks, and don't forget your emergency rations. In wintry conditions, make sure you carry or have the means to make a hot drink.
- Carry a simple first-aid and survival kit.
- Check that no one in your group has any injuries, medical problems or allergies.
- Be aware when darkness falls. Wear a watch. Carry a torch (with spare batteries and bulb).
- The standard distress signal is six blasts on a whistle in quick succession, repeated at one-minute intervals.
- Make sure you know the emergency drills and signals. Don't wave at helicopters – they might think you need assistance.

WALKING AND WALK-LEADING

Whether you are alone or in a group, the walk itself should find its own pace. To hurry it too much will cause members of the party to tire and not enjoy the experience. If the route is steep or rough then a slow pace is required; if flat, the pace can be quickened, the idea being to minimise the physical effort. Walking too fast and lifting the legs over rocky or steep ground all put strain on muscles and joints, causing tiredness and aches.

The best way to walk is to find a route and rhythm where you can swing the legs forward naturally, in time with the rest of the body, including the arms, to facilitate a smooth, well-balanced action. Arms and hands should be kept free, so that in the event of a slip or fall they can be used to protect yourself against serious injury.

However, the use of one or two walking poles is increasing in popularity, especially when carrying a heavy pack, and provides additional balance and stability when descending steep slopes or crossing streams. The walker should take into account the nature of the terrain and his own ability before deciding on using poles or keeping one or both hands free.

Take extra care when climbing or descending steep slopes, and avoid scree areas. Running too fast downhill is the easiest way to cause an injury.

AUTHOR'S NOTE

I must admit that I frequently walk alone – indeed, many walkers prefer to do so. However, this is generally not advisable, even if the individual concerned is experienced and has taken all the necessary precautions. If an accident or incident occurs, the lone walker has problems. The individual puts his own life at risk, as well as those of the rescue services.

Always observe right of way signs

GROUP LEADERS

Anyone who leads a group of hillwalkers should possess
the relevant experience and skills. These skills will be a
balance between time spent hillwalking and basic safety
procedures learnt from study, both in theory and in
practice. However, every member of the party should
have some basic knowledge, especially of safety
procedures and correct behaviour in potentially
dangerous situations. The party leader also needs to be
fit enough mentally and physically, to enable him to deal
with any unforeseen problems and pass on information
confidently to the other members.

Group leaders should choose a route that is suitable for all members

GROUPS OF HILLWALKERS

If you are planning a long or difficult trip, filling in a route card is essential. This details the route and the proposed timing of the trip. Once filled out, the card should be left with someone who will be able to get help if you are later back than you intended. For a shorter trip or with a small party, it is not as necessary to fill out a route card, but it is still imperative to let someone know your route and the time you hope to return.

When planning a route, take the terrain into consideration and allow the time accordingly. For example, a party on fairly level ground will walk at an average 5 km/h (3 mph).

However, hillwalkers will seldom find themselves
walking over flat ground for any length of time. It is
much more likely that they will be slogging uphill or
taking it easy downhill. In 1892 a Scottish hillwalker and
climber called Naismith advanced the following rule for
working out the duration of a walk and climb:

- If walking normally at 3 mph (5 km/h), add 30
  minutes extra for every 1000 ft (300 m) of ascent.

Going downhill also changes the speed and duration of
the walk, but in most cases the ascent and descent times
wil more or less balance out each other. On very steep
downhill slopes add 10 minutes for every 1000 ft (300 m)
of descent, but where the ground is gently sloping deduct
10 minutes for every 1000 ft (300 m) of descent.

The most important point to remember is that your
group should walk only as fast as the slowest member. In
this way you should be able to estimate the time it will
take you to cover the route and therefore set a deadline
for return. When considering the route, also remember
to take the appropriate compass bearings and look for
any escape routes or convenient shelters in the event of
an emergency.

The usual position for the leader of the party to walk is
in front, but this is by no means a hard and fast rule; it all
depends on the type of party, the type of terrain or even
the leader's own preference. Other members of the walk
should be encouraged to take the lead and plan various
legs in order to gain experience. What is important is
that everyone keeps together and that everyone in the

party knows where they are and where they are going at all times. No member of the party should ever go off on their own.

During a walk, the party will need a break every now and again. Here are a few points to take into consideration:

- Stop overlooking a scenic view.
- Check your map and compass.
- Keep breaks short, otherwise you will upset the natural rhythm of the walk.
- Only eat small amounts of food. A large meal can cause sickness.
- Check every member of the party is comfortable.
- Warn people you intend to move off a few minutes in advance.

GROUP MEMBERS

From a safety point of view it is important to restrict the amount of people in any one party. The ideal number in a party is about six, and it should be no more than ten if the route is long or hard. A minimum number is three, so that if a member of the party is injured or incapacitated, one of the others can stay with him, while the remaining member can go for help. It is also important to balance the fitness, age group and experience of your party, both from a safety and an enjoyment point of view. Trying to control the walking pace where the age of participants varies greatly will cause the group to become fragmented, as the older members will be unable to keep up with the younger ones. The same goes for differences in fitness and health.

CONTACTS FOR ADVICE ON WALKING

Most regions in Great Britain support numerous walking groups, details of which can be found in your local *Yellow Pages*, or, in many cases, at local libraries. Some groups walk purely for the joy of discovering the countryside and stay to the lowland paths and roads. These are great to join if you need to improve your walking fitness, as most of the walks do not involve climbing hills. Other groups are more adventurous and include cross-country routes and weekend camps. Whichever group you join you will find a wealth of knowledge and experience to draw on, but above all you will find people like yourself with a love of the great outdoors.

A list of addresses for various national organizations is given on page 191.

Rights of Way

Your right of access to walk over land in Britain will depend on a number of considerations. Usually, where there is a path regularly used by walkers there is no problem, but some routes do have limited access or need special permission to use them. It is always wise to check on the legal situation first. It should also be noted that access rights differ between England/Wales and Scotland.

AUTHOR'S NOTE

At the time of writing, new laws on access to the open countryside in England and Wales are being considered. The revision is by way of a Consultation Paper which is produced by the Department of the Environment, Transport and the Regions (DETR) and distributed to all interested bodies. These bodies have been asked to contribute their ideas so that through open discussion the government can come to a balanced conclusion. Copies of the Consultation Paper can be obtained by contacting: **DETR, Publications Despatch Centre, Blackhorse Road, London SE99 6TT. Tel: 0181 691-9191**

An equivalent process on rights of way is being undertaken by Scottish National Heritage. Recommendations will be forwarded to the new

Scottish Parliament, which will consider implementing any changes. Further information can be obtained from: **Scottish National Heritage, Recreation and Access Group, 2 Anderson Place, Edinburgh EH6 5NP. Tel: 0131 446-2469**

Powers in force at the time of writing include:

The National Parks and Access to the Countryside Act 1949

The Wildlife and Countryside Act 1981

Rights of Way Act 1990

EC Council Regulation 2078/92 (the Agri-Environment Regulation)

ENGLAND AND WALES

The most widely-known right to enjoy the countryside is that given by 'public rights of way'. All public rights of way are highways in law. Anyone may use a right of way, and may do so at any time. You should, of course, respect this freedom of use by other people, as you are entitled to expect that others will respect your own freedom of use. An up-to-date map will clearly indicate all rights of way.

You should not be intimidated or prevented from using a right of way. Providing you keep to the stipulated route and use a right of way properly you are exercising a right given to you by the law – not a privilege granted by the owner or occupier. It is reasonable to expect any right of way to be kept open, unobstructed and convenient to use.

It is important to realise, however, that a right of way gives only a right of passage to travel across the land. It does not entitle you to roam at will over the land, or to use the land or the path for other purposes. Remember too, that rights of way are normally just simple paths and tracks through a wood, across farmland or beside a stream. Many do not have a hard surface. They can often be muddy in winter or bordered by vegetation in summer. Sometimes a path may not be visible on the ground at all; you are still entitled to use it, but you may need a good map to be able to follow the correct line.

SCOTLAND

In Scotland the position on legal rights of way is less clear than in England and Wales. There are some similarities, however: like England and Wales, footpaths, bridleways and highways are considered public rights of way. For these to exist in law they have to have been in uninterrupted use for more than twenty years with the owner's express permission, connect two public places and follow a defined route. However, unlike England and Wales, the authorities do not usually keep records and it is quite often difficult to establish what is a public right of way and what is not. This is slowly changing as some local authorities are attempting to draw up definitive maps. The exceptions to the above are long-distance footpaths, which are signposted along their routes and are easily recognised as common-law rights of way.

In Scotland there is a concept known as 'right to roam', a public-enhanced belief that a walker has the right to walk wherever he pleases. In reality, this has no basis in law – if you trespass and claim the 'right to roam', the courts will not recognize your claim.

TYPES OF RIGHTS OF WAY

How a right of way can be used depends on what kind of highway it is:

- If the highway is a **footpath** it may be used only for walking.

- A **bridleway** may be used for riding or leading a horse, as well as walking. Riding a bike is also permitted, but driving a horse-drawn cart is not.

- A **byway** is open to all traffic from walkers to vehicles.

- A **public path** can be either a footpath or a bridleway.

WHAT YOUR RIGHTS ALLOW

When using a right of way to travel from place to place you can, of course, stop for a while to admire the view or take a photograph. Providing that you do not cause an obstruction you may sit down by the side of the path to rest or perhaps make a sketch. You may take a dog with you on a right of way, but you must ensure that it is kept on a lead and under control.

RESPONSIBILITIES FOR RIGHTS OF WAY

The main responsibility for rights of way falls on the highway authority. If the highway authority is a county council, there will also be a district council for the area. There may also be a local community council. District and community councils have important discretionary powers, allowing them to work with the highway authority to manage, protect and maintain rights of way. For example, a district council can maintain footpaths and bridleways, can act as the agent for the county council to carry out other functions, and can initiate its own orders to create, divert or extinguish public paths. Community councils can also maintain footpaths and bridleways. They can take action against anyone who unlawfully obstructs a right of way, or they can require the highway authority to act. They can insist that a path or byway is signposted where it meets a metalled road, or carry out their own signposting and waymarking with the consent of the highway authority. Some of the most important statutory duties that a highway authority has towards rights of way include:

- Asserting and protecting the public's rights to use and enjoy rights of way.
- Maintaining the surface of most public paths.
- Preventing, as far as possible, the stopping-up or obstruction of any highway.
- Ensuring that farmers comply with the law that paths over cultivated land are properly restored after they have been disturbed (e.g. by ploughing) and thereafter remain visible on the ground, and ensuring that farmers do not allow growing crops to inconvenience the use of any right of way.
- Preparing and keeping up to date a 'definitive map and statement', i.e. a formal, legal record of all rights of way.
- Signposting footpaths, bridleways and byways where they meet a metalled road and providing additional signs and waymarks wherever they are necessary.

A highway authority's discretionary powers allow it to:

- Create new paths by agreement with the landowner.
- Make orders to create, divert and extinguish public paths. Paths can be extinguished because of safety fears, new planning or because a new right of way has been established.

- Improve rights of way, for example by providing seats and street lighting.
- Provide footpath wardens.

Open access land can be enjoyed by all, but camping may be prohibited

OPEN COUNTRY ACCESS LAND

Under the Countryside Act of 1968, 'open country' is defined as land consisting wholly or predominantly of mountain, moorland, heath, down, cliff, foreshore and woodland, and land alongside canals, rivers and other stretches of water. There is usually legal public access to such areas in England, Wales and Scotland, although certain bylaws such as the prohibition of camping and camp fires may be in force. Details of such areas may be gained from the relevant local or national park authorities.

COMMON LAND

The origins of common land date back to the feudal systems of medieval times. These areas of open land were given over to the locals, or commoners, to graze their livestock or gather wood and brush for their fires. Since the Enclosure Acts of the 18th and 19th centuries, much common land has been lost, but where it has been retained the old rights of commoners still exist. Although on most common land there now exists a public right of access by foot, bylaws do exist to control certain activities. For example, camping, firelighting and driving a vehicle are prohibited on common land. Common land in Scotland is virtually nonexistent.

FORESTRY COMMISSION

As long as access does not pose any threat to its commercial interests, the Forestry Commission welcomes walkers onto its land free of charge. In some places it even provides facilities for visitors such as picnic areas and camping sites.

NATIONAL TRUSTS

The National Trust generally permits public access on foot freely at all times. However, once again, certain bylaws must be followed. There are sometimes areas which the Trust restricts to walkers because of agricultural expediency or to protect environmentally sensitive areas of conservation. The National Trust for Scotland has far more areas of unrestricted access and has chosen not to pass any bylaws on its land, preferring instead to give advice on environmentally sensitive areas.

COMMON PROBLEMS AND OBSTRUCTIONS

The responsibilities of the landowner and occupier are generally limited to respecting the public's rights of passage and to doing nothing that would inconvenience or endanger the public in any way. As most rights of way are over farmed land, provisions have been made concerning gates and stiles and to allow land to be cultivated.

STILES AND GATES

The variety of construction of stiles is part of the character of our footpaths. All stiles, gates and similar structures must be maintained in a safe condition and must not unreasonably interfere with the use of a right of way. A stile that is topped with barbed wire, or one that is dilapidated and difficult to use, and stiles or padlocked gates on a bridleway that obstruct the route for horse riders, are all unlawful and should be reported to the highway authority.

Stiles and gates are there for a purpose – use them properly

It is normally the landowner or occupier's duty to maintain gates and stiles in a safe condition. If they do this they can recover at least 25 per cent of the cost from the highway authority. If they do not, the highway authority can require the work to be done, or carry out the work itself and recover its costs. In practice, many authorities now provide free materials in the form of a stile or gate kit, which the farmer or volunteers can then install.

In repairing a stile or gate the farmer is not required to make the right of way any more convenient to use, for example by replacing a stile with kissing gates to help elderly people or by providing a dog latch to help less agile dogs. However, the highway authority or community council may be willing to arrange for such improvements to be carried out in agreement with the farmer. The highway authority's permission is normally required before a new stile or gate can be erected across a right of way. Putting a fence, including an electric fence, across a right of way without providing a satisfactory and safe means of crossing it would constitute an obstruction.

PLOUGHED PATHS AND GROWING CROPS

One common problem, encountered by anyone walking or riding in the countryside, is to find that the path they are following has been obliterated by ploughing or is covered by a growing crop. Important changes in the law were introduced in 1990 to help resolve these problems by making the farmer's rights and responsibilities much clearer. Highway authorities have a duty to enforce the new law and have been given strong powers do so. In addition to any prosecution they may bring, the authority can swiftly put matters right by entering onto the land and carrying out the necessary work, and then recovering its costs from the farmer.

If a footpath or bridleway runs around the edge of a field, its surface must not be ploughed or disturbed. Ploughing or disturbing the surface of a byway or public right of way is also prohibited, regardless of whether it runs along the edge of a field or across it.

If a footpath or bridleway runs across a field, and cannot conveniently be avoided, the farmer is entitled to plough or disturb it as and when it is necessary to do so to sow, cultivate or harvest a crop. He is then under a duty both to restore the surface of the path so as to make it reasonably convenient for walkers and riders to use, and to make sure that the line of the path is (and remains) apparent on the ground. Normally this must be carried out within twenty-four hours of the start of the disturbance. In the case of the first disturbance for any one crop, a longer period of fourteen days is allowed (to provide for the initial preparation of the land). Each period may be extended if agreed in advance with the highway authority.

The new law also deals with the problem of crops growing on or alongside rights of way. Crops must not be allowed to grow on, or to overhang, any footpath, bridleway or other right of way so as to inconvenience the public or prevent the line of the right of way from being apparent on the ground. 'Crops' includes cereals, oil seed rape and root crops, but does not include grass being grown for pasture, silage or haymaking.

Minimum widths are laid down for the farmer to work to, for example when restoring the surface of a footpath across a field or in keeping a right of way clear of growing crops. For rights of way across a field the minimum widths are 1 m (3 ft) for a footpath, 2 m (6 ft) for a bridleway and 3 m (9 ft) for other rights of way. At field edges, these widths are increased to 1.5 m (4 ft 6 in), 3 m (9 ft) and 5 m (15 ft) respectively.

You may find a right of way that is blocked (by fallen trees or rocks, barbed wire or rubbish, for example) or one that has become overgrown with vegetation. These can all be considered as obstructions and should be reported to the highway authority. The authority should clear natural obstructions as quickly as possible. It can order overhanging vegetation to be cut back, barbed wire close to a highway to be removed, and can clear anything placed or planted on the highway. If the authority has ordered an obstruction to be removed within a stated time and the obstruction is not removed within that period, the authority can remove it and recover the cost from the person concerned.

INTIMIDATION

If anyone prevents you from using a public right of way by telling you to leave, by keeping a fierce dog close to the highway to deter you or by any other form of intimidation or harassment, you should report the matter to the highways authority. If anyone uses or threatens to use force against you, you should also report the matter to the police. You may also be entitled to prosecute privately or to apply to the magistrates to have the offender bound over to keep the peace. Committing a breach of the peace, or behaving in a way likely to provoke one, is an offence for which the penalty on conviction is imprisonment, a fine or both.

INTIMIDATION BY A DOG

It may be that you are prevented from using a right of way due to the presence of a fierce dog, either with or without its owner present. Unleashed dogs, especially those on remote farms, may well run at you and snap at your heels or lower leg. Some dogs will bite into your clothing and maintain their grip; if this is the case, try offering a padded garment to the animal (such as a jacket) to prevent being bitten. A country dog will not normally stray far from its own territory – usually the farm gate – and you should avoid them if at all possible.

AUTHOR'S NOTE

If a dog is charging at you, try to break its momentum. This can be achieved by standing exposed next to some obstruction like a tree or the corner of a wall until the dog is a few feet away, and then at the last second moving rapidly behind the obstruction. The dog will be forced to slow in order to turn. Take advantage of this to lash out. If the owner is not present and you have no other way of defending yourself, try charging directly at the dog with your arms outstretched and screaming. Given the size of a human being in comparison to that of a dog, and the sudden unexpected nature of the attack, there is a good chance you will break the dog's spirit. A dog's confidence and security can be weakened very quickly, and while they may continue to bark, they should not come too close.

Your Dog

If you are planning to take your dog for a walk in the countryside, make sure that it does not become a menace either to other people or to those who manage the land. You can take a dog along a right of way but you must keep it under proper control at all times, just as you would in the town. You should not let it foul the right of way or farmland or any place that the public may use, and it is only common sense to watch your dog carefully on a bridleway where you may meet horses. If your dog injures a person, animal or property, you may be liable for damages.

You must be especially careful in any area where there is livestock. If your dog worries them it can have serious consequences; not only are you liable to be prosecuted and fined, but you may also be ordered to pay compensation and have the dog destroyed. You should note that 'worrying livestock' means attacking or chasing any farm animal or poultry. In a field or enclosure in which there are sheep, a dog that is not a working dog can be regarded as 'worrying livestock' simply by not being on a lead or otherwise under close control. A landowner can also shoot a dog that is apparently out of control and worrying sheep, and the owner of the dog will not be compensated.

Don't allow your dog to run through arable crops or to flush out game from hedgerows or scrub. Although the damage caused may seem trivial, such actions will not be appreciated by the farmer, and can easily harm wildlife, especially nesting birds.

BULLS AND CATTLE

A farmer should not keep a mature bull in a field enclosure over which there is a right of way. However, there are exceptions and it is possible that you may enter a field full of cattle which contains a bull. Grazing cattle will rarely attack people who are giving them a wide berth. However, certain young beasts may run towards you out of curiosity. Bulls have a different temperament and have in the past caused many deaths and serious injuries to hillwalkers and campers, either through carelessness or lack of respect for the bull's nature.

- Wherever possible, avoid going into any enclosed space or field that contains a bull, but if you have to go in, take into account the following points:
- Keep to the edges and keep the bull in your sight the whole time – never turn your back on it.
- Before entering an animal enclosure check for sign of any bulls.
- If you must pass by the herd, do so at a safe distance, moving carefully and quietly.
- If any cattle start to approach you, shouting and waving your arms can normally chase off young heifers.
- Check that you have some form of escape route open to you should a bull suddenly appear.
- Remember to close gates behind you whenever you are walking through fields where there is livestock.
- Keep any dog on a lead.

TRESPASS

If you enter someone else's land you will be trespassing unless you have permission to be there or some form of right of way to follow, such as a right conferred by the Act of Parliament. In either case there are likely to be conditions attached to the public's use of the land, and if you contravene these you will be trespassing.

Trespass is a criminal offence only in exceptional instances, so (except in one of these instances) you cannot be prosecuted simply for being in the wrong place at the wrong time. However, if you cause loss or damage you can be prosecuted (and fined) or sued (and be made to pay compensation) or both.

If you trespass persistently the landowner or occupier can seek a court injunction to keep you out. If you do find yourself trespassing and a landowner or occupier asks you to leave or to return to the footpath, you should do so. You must be allowed to do so freely. If you fail to leave, then, depending on the circumstances, the use of reasonable force to make you leave may be justifiable.

Instances in which trespass is a criminal offence include trespass on railway and Ministry of Defence land. In addition, a law designed to deal with the problem of new-age travellers makes it an offence in certain circumstances for two or more people to take up residence on any land. In some cases, such as on some commons and local authority land, you can be prosecuted if you break the local bylaws. Remember that in Scotland, invoking the 'right to roam' is not a sufficient defence against trespassing.

If you trespass you do so at your own risk. Even so, trespassers may sue for damages for injuries sustained as a result of any deliberate attempt to injure them, or through reckless disregard for their safety. Certainly, trespassers must not be injured deliberately or threatened, and if, for example, a landowner was out shooting and continued shooting even though there was good reason to believe a trespasser might be injured, the trespasser could claim damages for any resulting injury. If the landowner threatened the trespasser with a firearm, the landowner would be committing a criminal offence.

ELECTRIC FENCES

Electric fences are increasingly used to contain farm animals. There are many types, including single-wire fences (often running alongside a conventional hedge or wall as a 'scare wire'), electrified nylon netting, low 'grass fences' of two parallel wires each just above the ground, and permanent electrified fences of four or five strands. There are even electric gates. They all work by sending a pulse of current along the wire every second or so. They are designed not to be dangerous, even though they may be powered by mains electricity. But they can still be very unpleasant if you touch them. You should be particularly careful not to get entangled in them. Be sure to keep your dog well away.

An electric fence alongside a public road or path should be identified with yellow warning signs at frequent intervals. Safe crossing posts should be provided on rights of way by a non-electrified gate or stile with the wires insulated, and the fence on either side also marked by warning signs. Barbed wire should never be electrified, nor should any metal that is not part of the fence itself, such as the hand rail on a bridge. If you find that any of these safety precautions are not being observed, report the matter to the highway authority or the Health and Safety Executive at once.

AUTHOR'S NOTE

If you are not sure if an electric fence is active or not, it is a wise precaution to check. This is simply done by placing a small blade of grass against the fence, making sure you do not directly touch the fence with any part of your body. Hold the blade of grass in your hand and touch the tip to the fence. If you feel nothing, advance the blade of grass, bringing your hand closer to the fence. If by the time your hand is within 15 mm (0.5 in) of the fence, you still feel no tingling sensation, the fence is not live.

Touching a blade of grass on an electric fence will indicate if the fence is active

CROP-SPRAYING

Spraying with pesticides and other chemicals is a widely-used method of protecting crops. The chemicals used to eliminate weeds, insects and fungal diseases can be dangerous to people. There are strict controls on the chemicals that are available and the way they can be used, and anyone using chemicals has a number of statutory obligations placed on them. They must ensure that the public is not endangered by posting warning signs on gates to fields that are to be sprayed. Further information should be given if there is any likelihood of the public picking fruit from plants, bushes, etc. where the spraying has taken place.

For your own safety, do not touch or interfere with any spraying equipment (whether or not it is in use) or with chemical containers, including any that are empty. It is best to avoid walking through crops that you know or suspect have been sprayed very recently, nor should you eat, drink or smoke in the area, or pick any fruit.

If, despite these precautions, you believe that you have been contaminated, then it is usually sufficient to wash any exposed skin in plenty of clean water. Change your clothes as soon as you can and rinse them separately. If the farmer is in the area, ask for advice about the chemicals being used. Should any symptoms subsequently develop, such as trouble with your eyes, feeling sick or difficulty with breathing, seek medical advice as soon as possible. Report any problems you encounter with crop-spraying both to the highway authority and the Health and Safety Executive.

ANIMAL DISEASE

You should not attempt to enter or walk across an area of land that you know to be contaminated by animal disease. You may not be putting yourself at risk, but the damage of transmitting the disease from one place to another and thus infecting clean animals is very high. The Ministry of Agriculture has the right to declare any area of land restricted if there has been an occurrence on that land of any serious communicable animal disease. In particular, foot-and-mouth disease can cause such a restriction, as happened in the late 1960s. In these cases even public rights of way are off limits and entering into such an area becomes a serious offence.

GAME-SHOOTING

There are areas in Great Britain where game-shooting may take place, and where access may be restricted on certain days of the year. Hillwalkers need to be aware of these dangers which are always publicly announced far in advance, and by seeking advice from the national park authorities.

The Mountaineering Council of Scotland, in association with the Scottish Landowners Federation, has published a list of estates and contact telephone numbers where information about deer-stalking should be available. While no stalking is carried out on Sundays, some estates still try to restrict access then as well. Areas owned by the National Trust for Scotland are much less restrictive during the stalking season and information is more freely available.

Private estates which own land where commercial hunting is carried out should also be sought out for advice on restricted areas during the shooting season. Legally recognised public rights of way are still free to be used even in an area in current use for game-stalking. However, in the interest of your own safety they are best avoided.

Shooting seasons are:

- Stags (mainly Scottish Highlands), 1 July–20 October
- Hinds (mainly Scottish Highlands), 21 October–15 February
- Grouse (moorland areas), 12 August–10 December

MILITARY TRAINING AREAS

Almost all military training areas are clearly marked on Ordnance Survey maps as 'Danger Areas'. Most ranges, both 'live-firing' and dry combat activity, are in constant

Avoid military training areas whenever possible

use and the hillwalker is best avoiding them, added to which many are out of bounds during any military manoeuvres. Many access points are manned by soldiers and where they are not, standard warning notices will be displayed, with red flags being flown during the day and red lights being displayed at night. Few of these areas clash with popular walking trails, but where they do you should consult the Range Liaison Officer.

Most military training areas are well established, which means that a large amount of ordnance has been fired over the years. Some of this may have misfired and not been found or disposed of safely. Should you walk across a military training area, do not be tempted to pick up or touch any device you find lying on the ground, no matter how small. Likewise, do not throw stones at a foreign object or attempt to dig it up.

FIRES

Most forest and moorland fires are started by people, whether accidentally or deliberately. They cause extensive damage to vegetation, threaten wildlife and livestock, and put human lives at risk. During dry periods extra care should be taken not to start a fire accidentally. Ensure that you do not discard any cigarette ends or matches, broken glass or bottles. Also, do not light a camp fire or camping stove unless it is safe to do so and completely under control. Before leaving a site, check that all firebeds are cold and dowse them with water.

Remember that some rights of access such as those allowed by the National Trust may be withdrawn in certain areas when there is a very high risk of fire. Adequate warning notices will be displayed in this eventuality.

LITTER

It goes without saying that responsible hillwalkers do not leave litter behind them. It is not only unpleasant for everyone else but can also be a source of danger and contamination to wildlife. When a trip is organised, plan for how much 'litter' you will be carrying back with you and how you will carry it back. On no account leave it behind, no matter how well hidden you think it will be.

Take all litter home or dispose of it in a proper bin

CAIRNS AND STONE PILES

For many years hillwalkers were encouraged to place a stone on a cairn as they passed to help build up a feature or landmark. The appearance of cairns is beginning to ruin the wilderness feeling of many routes, so don't add to them.

Man-made cairns serve little purpose – do not add to them

TREES, PLANTS AND WILD ANIMALS

As hillwalkers we are merely passing through the
countryside, but its wealth of wild trees and plants are the
food and homes to many wild animals. Hillwalkers need
to be aware of the animals in their walking environment
and try to keep any disturbance down to a minimum.
This is particularly true of birds in the nesting season. A
disturbed bird may leave the nest only to return when the
chicks have died of cold or hunger, or sometimes it may
never return at all. Dogs should be kept under control at
all times but particularly when there are wild animals
around. While you are encouraged to admire the
beautiful variety of flora and fauna, it is illegal to pick or

uproot any wild plants without the permission of the landowner, and some are protected by law.

AUTHOR'S NOTE

In today's technological age, few people know or even bother to recognise and name a type of tree or species of wild plant. Carrying a small book on the subject, such as Gem Trees or Gem Wild Flowers, adds extra interest for any hillwalker, and leads to a better understanding of nature's bounty.

Stick to the designated pathway and prevent further erosion

EROSION

Erosion is becoming a real problem as popular footpaths feel the weight of many heavily-booted walkers, causing major problems of soil compaction and erosion. When the grass and vegetation is destroyed, the structure of the underlying soil can become unstable and will wash away in the next heavy downpour. When the path becomes so eroded, it becomes difficult to walk on and so walkers detour off it. This then sets up the same cycle of destruction on a new piece of land until sometimes a large area can be affected. No matter how tempting it is to walk on fresh ground, stick to the footpath, and, if possible, try to tread on stones rather than soil.

DAMAGE TO WALLS AND GATES

Usually, footpaths across boundaries have stiles or gates and these should be used in preference to climbing stone walls. Dry-stone walls are easily damaged, which means that livestock could escape, as well as presenting the landowner with a costly repair job. If there is no alternative to climbing a wall, ensure that any stones knocked off are replaced. Just as importantly, if you do use a gate, make sure that you close and fasten it firmly behind you. If a gate or stile is damaged, it should be reported to the farmer or local council.

CONSERVATION

It is vital for hillwalkers to treat the countryside with respect and be aware that some areas are environmentally sensitive, easily disturbed or destroyed. It is up to each generation to protect what we have inherited and not to spoil our wonderful countryside for future walkers. Make yourself aware of the environment and the impact you may have upon it.

Clothing, Boots and Walking Equipment

Man is a tropical animal and needs clothes to protect himself against the British weather. The human body functions best between 96 °F and 102 °F; above or below this range, the person may start to decline in health. Therefore, the maintenance of body temperature and the prevention of injury are just as important to a hillwalker as the consumption of food or drinking water. Climatic temperature, wind, moisture loss, illness and shock can affect body temperature. Conduction, convection, radiation, evaporation, respiration and wind can cause heat loss or gain. This last factor is by far the worst threat in any situation, as wind chill can kill very quickly. In cold and wet conditions it can rob the body of heat, and in hot conditions it can rob the body of moisture.

Most hillwalkers will tell you that getting the right mixture of clothing to suit the British climate, especially in such extreme environments as hills and mountains, can be a fruitless task. The weather can change from hot sun to wet, biting cold rain in a matter of hours. Therefore, it is necessary to be prepared for all eventualities, so that in an emergency you will have a greater chance of survival. To guard against these factors wear protective clothing, and providing your choice of clothing is correct you should be comfortable, snug and safe.

OVERHEATING AND SWEATING

Even in cold weather it is possible to overheat, especially while wearing layered clothing. Bloodflow helps to distribute heat round the body, so be aware of any tight or restrictive clothing that may hinder this. If you're wearing more than one layer in the case of gloves and socks, make sure that the outer layer is comfortably large enough to fit over the inner. If you find yourself overheating, first of all loosen the clothing at neck, wrists and waist. If this isn't enough, start to take off your outer layers of clothing, one layer at a time. As soon as you stop exercising or working, you should put these clothes on again or you will become chilled. If the weather is wet remove one of the inner layers, always maintaining a waterproof outer layer.

HOW THE LAYER SYSTEM WORKS

The type of clothing and how you wear it will determine your body temperature. Using several thin layers will keep you far warmer than one thick layer, as they trap the warm air produced by the body. Additionally, by adding or removing a layer one is able to control the body's

The layer system keeps you warm without overheating

heat. If you are exerting yourself by walking at a swift pace, be aware that you will sweat and that the sweat will not only make your clothing wet, thereby exposing you more to the cold, but that it will also degrade the fibres of the fabric. So when doing strenuous exercise, remove some of your underlayers, replacing them once you have stopped. That way you will always have a dry layer next to your skin.

Your underclothes, that is those next to your skin, should be made of a thin, cotton material – something like a loose-fitting thermal cotton vest. This layer will absorb perspiration, thereby removing excess moisture from the skin. It is important that this layer is changed daily and washed.

The next layer should ideally be a garment that can be fastened at the neck and wrists, thereby trapping the warm air – for example, a thick woollen shirt or zip-up collar-type sweater.

A third layer should consist of a fleece-type jacket that can be easily removed when the body begins to overheat.

Finally, choose an outer garment that is wind- and, if possible, waterproof. This could be made from tightly-woven cotton, polycotton, fibre-pile material or nylon. It should be fitted with a good hood protecting as much of the head and face as possible. Garments made from such materials as Gore-Tex are excellent as they allow trapped vapour to permeate through the fabric and reduce overheating.

HEAD, HANDS AND FEET

The head is important in both cold and hot weather as it is particularly vulnerable to heat loss. An uncovered head will lose up to a third of body heat, but this can be prevented by wearing a head-over (a knitted woollen tube worn around the neck) or scarf, which can be removed from time to time in order to prevent overheating. Although most waterproof outers have some form of hood attached, it is still advisable to wear protective headwear in cold conditions.

In hot weather an uncovered head can cause the body to overheat and succumb to heatstroke, as well as suffer from sunburn. Wearing a soft, wide-brimmed hat will provide protection and prevent this.

Feet and hands are at the extremities of the circulation system and so are in danger of frostbite and other unpleasant conditions caused by the cold and wet. Feet can be looked after by ensuring your boots are watertight before setting off. However, make sure that you do not overdo the layers on your feet as this will hinder circulation and make the problem worse. The same goes for boots that are laced too tightly. To make sure that the circulation in your feet is working properly, keep moving and wiggle your toes every now and again. Check for any signs of numbness as this is an indicator that your foot's blood supply is being trapped. At the first opportunity change your wet socks for dry ones.

The hands need protecting from the cold and wet, and unless fully waterproof, gloves have a tendency to get very wet. In poor weather conditions cold and wet hands inhibit your ability to fend for yourself. Even small tasks such as doing up a zip become impossible. Always carry at least one pair of good loose-fitting gloves. However, unless you need to use your fingers you may prefer to use mittens. Mittens will warm your hands far quicker than gloves owing to the amount of air circulating around your hand. If your gloves get wet a spare pair of thick socks placed over the hands will help to protect them.

KEEPING CLOTHING IN GOOD REPAIR

Dirty or ripped clothing does not provide good insulation from or protection against the elements; don't let your walking clothes fall into disrepair. The Eskimos have a very good habit of repairing clothing as soon as it becomes damaged, thereby reducing any further deterioration and maintaining the garment's effectiveness. It is good to adopt this bit of wisdom, especially where windproof outer garments are concerned. Never discard your clothing on a walk, no matter how warm it may feel at the beginning or how heavy and cumbersome the clothes are becoming. Never cut up your clothing for the sake of comfort. It may be hot for a few days but don't be tempted to cut the bottoms off your trousers in order to make them into shorts. The same applies to shirt sleeves.

Long-term wear and tear will take its toll on any clothing, no matter how good it is. If you allow dirt to build up on your clothes, it will destroy the fibres and reduce the effectiveness of the garments. It is essential to keep your clothes clean. Washing them is the best way. If this is not practicable, a daily shaking or beating will do. Clothes worn next to the body, especially socks and underclothing, will need frequent washing and daily attention – this is essential to your health and hygiene. Many native tribes clean their clothes by simply soaking them in water and beating them against rocks. If you choose to do this, take care not to damage any buttons and zips.

When clothing gets wet, for example through perspiration or rain, its insulation properties are reduced and it will lose heat up to twenty-five times faster than dry clothing. If clothes do get wet, make every effort to dry them. This can be done by draping them over clean rocks to be warmed by the sun, or by hanging them from tree branches to dry in the wind. If possible, build a fire and dry them by that, but never leave them unattended or you might burn them. Take special care when drying leather boots or gloves by a fire. Leather, if dried too fast, has a tendency to stiffen and crack.

In sub-zero temperatures, wet clothing can be hung up to freeze. The moisture turns into ice particles that can then be beaten out. This works best with tightly-woven garments.

SURVIVAL CLOTHING

The greatest danger to hillwalkers in Britain is getting wet in a cold and windy environment, resulting in the rapid loss of body heat, leading to hypothermia, and a swift death if unprepared. Survival clothing can be summed up in three words: plastic bags, newspapers and cardboard. If you have prepared yourself properly and included in your preparations a small survival kit you should have enclosed a large plastic bag. In an emergency, this can easily be converted into a full-length waterproof coat. This can be done in two ways:

- Cut a small slit in the bottom for your head to pass through.
- Cut a small aperture where your face will be if you drop the bag over your head. There is no need to cut side holes for the arms – simply keep them inside and dry.

The countryside is littered with plastic sacks and discarded supermarket bags – utilize them to protect your hands and feet. Dry cardboard or newspapers make excellent insulation to tuck around your body (always protect the chest area first), and if you need to sit on wet, cold ground use a layer of plastic or cardboard. You may end up looking like a tramp, but such improvised clothing will help keep you alive.

The most important points to remember with regard to hillwalking clothing are:

- Keep clothing clean.
- Avoid overheating and sweating.
- Keep clothing dry.
- Repair damage to clothing immediately.
- Improvise in an emergency.

BOOTS AND FOOTWEAR

The right footwear is like an old friend – it never rubs you up the wrong way and supports you when the going gets tough. A healthy pair of feet and good footwear are major requirements for those participating in any outdoor walking activity. The fact that we carry our entire body weight on two feet instead of four, like most animals, means that we place pressure on our feet. This is especially true when we are also carrying the additional weight of a heavy rucksack while walking over rough terrain. It is therefore important

Good, comfortable walking boots are an essential item

that you look after both your feet and your boots. Failure to do so could easily mean not completing your walk, no matter how fit the rest of your body is.

SELECTING FOOTWEAR

As a general rule, you should choose a pair of walking boots that combines lightness with adequate support and protection. Boots can come in a bewildering array of styles and suitabilities for different terrains. Good boots are often quite expensive, so most hillwalkers can only afford to possess one pair. Invariably, this pair has to be able to cope with all kinds of environmental conditions and terrains.

Boots are made for just about every purpose. Some are better for rugged climbing, others for day walking, some are lighter and cooler for summer, others heavier and insulated for winter weather. It is up to the individual hillwalker to assess his own needs and choose a boot that provides the best compromise for the type of walking he expects to do.

Socks are also important; lightweight fabric boots are designed to be worn with a single sock, while heavier boots may require two pairs of socks. In the latter case, the inner sock should be lightweight wool or silk for warmth, while the outer sock should have thickness to cushion the foot.

Things you should look out for when purchasing a new pair of walking boots:

- Always wear the same type of socks in which you would go walking. Make sure your toes are not touching the end of the boot. A good-fitting boot should feel comfortable, but not restrictive.

- Examine the boot construction and weight. (New leather boots normally need a frequent and liberal coating with wax, but they offer better support than fabric boots.)

- The boot backstay should protect and support the boot, as should the heel corner and toecap.

- The boot should be high enough to protect the ankle, with a padded scree collar and a bellows tongue to protect against water and debris.

- Both the insole and upper lining should be well-cushioned, giving a firm but comfortable fit to the entire foot.

- The boot should be waterproof.

- A good grip is essential, especially on wet, slippery rocks. Try to avoid PVC – choosing a rubber star-patterned sole will give you much better grip. The sole thickness will depend upon the sort of terrain on which you propose to walk. General hillwalking does not require an extremely stiff sole, as in mountaineering. Try twisting the sole to see if it is flexible. If it twists easily it will not give much support during a fall.

- Try to stand on an incline, or tap the heel and toe of your boot. If the toes feel trapped, try the next size up.

- Never purchase new footwear if you have any form of foot ailment such as ingrown toenails or corns. Wait until they have been treated.

Footwear Maintenance

It takes time to get used to a new set of boots, so start by wearing them with the laces slightly slack and always make sure the tongue is neatly flat against the insole of your foot. Wear them around the house or go for short walks – this should iron out any hot-spots before you go hillwalking.

Once purchased, careful maintenance will allow you to get a long life out of your boots. Clean mud from them at every opportunity then wash and polish or spray them. Any detachable insoles and wet laces should be removed and dried thoroughly using either the sun or another heat-source. Beware though, of putting wet boots too close to an open fire, as leather tends to crack when it dries too fast. Instead, dry them out by stuffing them with an absorbent material, such as paper or tissue, and leave them in a warm place. Once the boots are dry, apply several layers of a good waterproof compound, making sure that each layer is well rubbed in. Regular and careful care will prolong the active life of your boots.

Boots are expensive and a comfortable pair is hard to replace. Using gaiters that cover the entire boot will help prolong the boots' active life. This is particularly so in snowy conditions as gaiters will prevent most of the snow from going down your boots.

RUCKSACKS

Your rucksack should be large enough to contain everything you need for both planned contingencies and unplanned survival situations. This will include some form of shelter, sleeping bag, clothes, food and water. You should consider your rucksack to be your outdoor home and, like any well-kept home, everything should be serviceable, clean and in its correct place.

Rucksacks have changed in recent years, providing a level of comfort, stability and versatility to suit every kind of outdoor activity. The past decade has seen the amalgamation of technical design and modern materials such as textured nylon, two-ply polycotton and Cordura to produce an almost limitless range of high-quality rucksacks and daypacks.

Choose a rucksack that best suits your walking requirements

Most rucksacks fall into three main categories, and within each category you will find a vast selection of makes and models to choose from. You should ask yourself what you intend to do with the pack. Once you have made this decision, you should evaluate the rucksacks available in that category.

SMALL DAYPACKS

These are designed for single-day use and are ideal if you want to carry basic day necessities such as your lunch, spare clothing, waterproofs, camera, etc. Sizes range from 18 litres to 40 litres and your own personal preference and needs should be taken into consideration. Daypacks come in different shapes and sizes, with various combinations of pockets and compartments in which to stow equipment. You would be well advised to choose a rucksack of simple construction if it is for day use only.

SPECIALIST PACKS

These are rucksacks designed for specialized use, such as climbing, mountain biking, fell-running, etc. They are for the most part soft and flexible, providing minimal resistance to body movement, although some larger packs do incorporate a very simple flexible frame which helps support the pack and its contents. Sizes for these packs are determined by the activity for which they are intended, but generally they are less than 30 litres.

FRAMED PACKS

This is a general type of rucksack which is used by those people who intend to spend time in the outdoors, i.e. camping. Framed packs have vastly improved in recent years, with the cumbersome external frames being replaced by internal supportive structures. This makes the framed pack much more comfortable without losing its stability. Most framed packs are adjustable, allowing the wearer to tailor the pack's back-length to different clothing and walking conditions. Most people in the United Kingdom rarely stay more than two nights in a tent encampment before they encounter civilization, and this should be taken into consideration when selecting the rucksack size – 50 litres to 70 litres is appropriate for a good backpacking holiday.

RUCKSACKS AND WEIGHT

The spinal column supports the upper body and transfers weight downwards to the pelvis. It does this by way of a series of curves which absorb shocks and allow flexibility. The major curve is the hollow in the lower back known as the lordosis. This curve acts as a spring to take the strain, and as a result it is prone to backache. A rucksack should be designed to fit in with the body shape, bear the weight it is intended to carry and remain stable. Good hip features on the rucksack, such as a wide, well-padded waist belt, help reduce the amount of strain placed on the lordosis curve. The rucksack's centre of gravity should be high on your back and most of its weight should be distributed between the shoulders and the hips. This way, your legs will help to bear the weight and your back will not get strained.

FITTING YOUR PACK

Once you have selected your rucksack, persuade the retailer to let you fill it with some weight. This is to assess how the various adjustments found on most rucksacks react to your individual body height and build. You should also be wearing appropriate clothing. Adjust the back-length and fit any chest and waist harness, then walk around the store, checking if the pack feels right. Rucksacks vary in price and quality – always try several different makes within your budget.

When buying a new rucksack, keep in mind the following points:

- What will be the main use for the pack?
- What size do you require?
- Does the pack fit well? If it doesn't, don't buy it.
- Check out all the features, especially the load-bearing areas.
- Ask the retailer to put some weight in the pack and have a little walk around.
- Check for any pressure spots, soreness or irritation and adjust the rucksack accordingly.

PACKING A RUCKSACK

Knowing how to pack a rucksack correctly is a skill that should be learnt before setting out on walks. The most important aspect is deciding what is essential and what is nonessential. Pack a rucksack well and you should be able to carry everything you need in comfort. There is only one tried and tested method which works and that is based on the principle that you should be able to get to all your equipment with the minimum of effort.

Items needed while you are walking, e.g. water, tea, flasks and snacks, should be in the side pockets. If the weather is hot and you intend to use some form of camel hydration system (a tube-and-water-container contraption which allows the walker to drink without stopping), fit it in one of the side pockets. Items of clothing needed for foul weather should be kept neatly folded under the rucksack top flap. Items for use at a specific time, e.g. sleeping bag, should be in the bottom of your rucksack, with those items that you will use frequently closer to the top.

Rain soaks through most rucksack material and makes it heavy. You could end up carrying an extra couple of kilograms in a rainstorm. Waterproof your rucksack, and seal all clothes and porous items in plastic bags.

Navigation

Having a sure knowledge of navigation techniques will certainly help a walker to avoid ending up in a potentially dangerous situation. This section outlines how a walker can navigate by map and compass or global positioning system, as well as by more improvised (and therefore less accurate) means.

There are three ways in which one can navigate: a map and compass; a global positioning system (GPS); or by using the sun, moon and stars. The correct use of a map and compass is a basic skill that every hillwalker can build upon until he is fully competent in navigational techniques. Other navigational skills, not dependent on a map and compass, can also be learnt and are extremely useful in survival situations. These basic skills will prove useful if your compass or GPS gets lost or damaged.

A map is an essential tool to help you plan and follow a route

ORDNANCE SURVEY MAPS

A map is an essential tool to help you plan and follow a route through the countryside. Sometimes it may be difficult to see the route of a right of way on the ground, but with the aid of a good map you should be able to follow it. Although there are a number of good local walking guides, many of which contain suitable maps, Ordnance Survey (OS) maps are recommended because they show such a variety of land features as well as rights of way.

The most useful OS map to help you enjoy the countryside is a 1:25,000 scale Pathfinder map. The scale is large enough to show public rights of way in green, and other helpful information such as field boundaries. For some areas of attractive countryside, 1:25,000 scale Outdoor Leisure maps have been produced, which show additional information, such as waymarked routes, camp sites, permissive paths and some areas of open access. The 1:50,000 scale Landranger map also shows most public rights of way (in red) but does not go into as much detail as the larger-scale Pathfinder.

As well as showing those public rights of way that are on the definitive maps, OS maps show other roads, tracks and paths. Not all of these are open to the public and the map therefore states 'the representation on this map of any other road, track or path is no evidence of the existence of a right of way'. In practice, it is usually safe to assume that you can drive, walk or ride along those roads and lanes that are shown in colour on the maps, unless there are clear notices to the contrary. Some minor lanes and tracks are shown uncoloured; for this reason they are sometimes known as 'white roads'. It will usually be obvious, either from the map or on the ground, whether a particular lane or track is public or private; for example, if it leads solely to a country house or to a farm it will normally be private. Ask the local authority for advice if you are unsure.

Altitude and relief on a map are shown using a series of contour lines, which join points equal height above sea level. Contour lines combine an accurate indication of height and a good indication of shape, and are generally shown on maps as continuous brown lines. When planning a route it is possible to follow some contour lines in order to keep a line of march at a consistent level.

COMPASS

A compass is a precision instrument used for navigation. They come in a variety of shapes and sizes, but all work on the principle of a magnetized needle which always points North. A 'Silva'-type compass is the most popular with hillwalkers as it lends itself to the map in a variety of ways. Most models are made of clear plastic with the compass

Compass work is a skill every hillwalker must learn

housing containing the magnetic needle offset to the left-hand side. The base of the compass has a magnifying glass and is etched with a variety of scales. The rim of the compass housing, which can be rotated, is marked with segments showing degrees, mils, or both, while printed on the base are an arrow and orienteering lines.

Always remember that any compass works on the magnetic attraction situated close to the North Pole. Local power supplies or heavy metal objects can pull the needle from its correct course. Most compass manufacturers dampen the movement of the needle by filling the compass housing with a liquid, which sometimes produces a bubble. Providing the bubble is not large it should not affect the compass's operation.

Most compasses come with the base scale marked either in degrees or mils, or both. In a full circle there are 360° or 6400 mils. Many people in the UK, including the navy and the airforce, favour degrees, while the army prefers to work in mils. In essence it makes little difference which measurement system is used, as they both operate in exactly the same way. However, the conversion table below should help you if you do need to swap between the two sets of measurements:

- 1° (degree) = 17.8 mils
- 1′ (minute) = 0.3 mils
- 1 mil = 3.4 minutes

ORIENTATING A MAP

When out on the hills it is important to know where you are in relation to the surrounding landscape. This can be done by using just a map, or by using a map and compass. The procedure is known as orientating or setting the map.

SETTING A MAP BY INSPECTION

Look for an obvious and permanent landmark, for example a river, road or mountain. Find the feature on the map and then simply align the map to the landmark. The map is now set to conform to the surrounding features.

SETTING THE MAP BY COMPASS

Setting the map by inspection

Pick one of the blue or black North–South gridlines on your OS map and lay a flat edge of the compass along it. Then, holding the map and compass together, turn both until the compass needle points North. The map is now set to conform to the surrounding features.

FINDING A GRID REFERENCE

A grid reference is a six-figure number which enables a map-reader to located an exact point on a map. When you look at a map, you will see it is covered in equally-spaced horizontal and vertical lines. These are called gridlines and on OS 1:50,000 and 1:25,000 maps they represent points which are 1 km apart. On Landranger maps the gridlines are blue and on Pathfinder maps the gridlines are black. The vertical lines are called eastings: these are always given first in grid references. The horizontal lines are called northings: these are given after the eastings. Each grid square is defined by the numbers straddling the left gridline of the easting and the centre bottom of the northing. For example, the illustrated grid square reads 1562.

A six-figure grid reference is obtained by subdividing a grid square

A six-figure grid reference is worked out in the following way:

- Locate the point for which you would like to provide a grid reference.
- Mentally divide the grid square in which your chosen point is located into ten equal parts along its left-hand and bottom gridline edges. Halfway across the square would therefore be 5.
- Note the number of the gridline to the left of the

chosen point, and then the number of the gridline below the chosen point. In the illustrated example these are 15 and 62.

- Working across the grid square from the left, ascertain how far across the square the chosen point is and convert its position into tenths.

- Repeat this procedure but this time working up the square to the chosen point from the gridline below.

- Placing the 'tenths' after the gridline numbers will give the easting reading followed by the northing, and therefore a six-figure grid reference for your chosen point which will be accurate to within 100 m on the ground.

- In the illustrated example the final grid reference is 155628.

MAGNETIC VARIATION

You should always bear in mind that when you talk about North, you could well be talking about one of three different Norths. These are:

Grid North. This is defined by the vertical gridlines shown on a map.

True North. This is the fixed location of the North Pole.

Magnetic North. This is a region in the north of Canada with a stron magnetic attraction, to which the needle on any compass will always point. However, this magnetic field is not stable and the direction of Magnetic North will vary by a small fraction from year to year, due to the movement in this magnetic field. The annual rate of change can be calculated from information which is printed in the top margin of all OS maps. You will need to know the printing date of the map and the annual rate of change of the magnetic field in order to calculate the correct current magnetic variation. Remember that the variation calculated will be that between Magnetic North and Grid North.

For example, if a map was printed in 1992, the angle between Grid and Magnetic North at that time 2° 30' (45 mils), and the annual rate of change is 3' (1 mil) east, the calculation would be as follows:

1992 to 1998 is six annual changes, meaning that in this case Magnetic North moved by 18' (6 mils) east towards Grid North. With an original angle of 2° 30' (45 mils), the change should be subtracted from the original difference of 2° 30' to give a magnetic variation of 2° 12' (39 mils).

To convert an original bearing, either add or subtract the variation. The following is useful to remember:

- **Mag to Grid = Get Rid**, i.e. subtract the variation from your compass bearing before applying it to the map.

- **Grid to Mag = Add**, i.e. add the variation to your map bearing before applying it to your compass.

TAKING A COMPASS BEARING FROM THE MAP

Once you have established where you are and where you wish to go, you should work out your route. Study the map and the distance. Plot the most logical route to your objective, taking into account the terrain and any obstacles. Divide up your route into legs, finishing each leg close to a prominent feature, i.e. a roadbridge, triangulation pillar or even the corner of a forest area. Take a bearing from where you are (call this point A) to the feature at the end of your first leg (call this point B). To do this, place one edge of the compass along the line adjoining A and B, making sure that the direction of travel arrow on the compass is pointing the way you want to go. Hold the compass plate firmly in position and rotate the compass dial so that the lines engraved in the dial base are parallel to the North–South gridlines on the map. Finally, read off the bearing next to the line of the direction of travel arrow on the compass housing. To walk on this bearing, simply keep the magnetic arrow pointing North over the etched arrow in the base and follow the line of the direction of travel arrow.

The bearing gives the direction to a certain point. It can be defined as the number of degrees in an angle measured clockwise from a fixed North–South gridline (an easting). The bearing for North is always zero. Compasses have scales of 360 degrees, or 6400 mils, in a full circle. Some compasses have both scales.

KEEPING ON COURSE

Three factors will determine which route you take: the weather; the time of day; and what the terrain is like between you and your final destination. In good visibility, select features which are both prominent on your map and visible to the eye. Once you have taken a bearing, choose a visible ground feature along the line of march and head towards it. This saves you constantly looking at your compass. It will also help keep you on course if the terrain pushes you off track, i.e. if you are forced to contour or avoid some obstacle. Ultimate success in reaching your final goal will depend on your route selection and not becoming a slave to your compass. Mistakes in poor visibility can be avoided if you consult the map every time you meet a prominent feature. Careful study of the map should provide you with a mental picture of the ground relief, which will in turn warn you of any obstacles, such as a river or marshland.

AUTHOR'S NOTE

There is a tendency during fog or poor visibility to wander downhill when you are contouring (moving round a mountain or across a steep slope by keeping at the same height). Every 100 m (300 ft) or so, take a few steps uphill to compensate for this. Don't forget that you will move more slowly in poor visibility.

PUTTING A COMPASS BEARING ON THE MAP

If you become disorientated, here is a simple way to pinpoint your position. This is done by locating a couple of landmarks which can also be identified on the map. Point the compass at the first landmark and, holding it steady, turn the housing until the direction of travel arrow is aligned with the magnetic needle. Now read off the bearing to the landmark. For example, say the bearing was 323° (5700 mil). Calculate the magnetic variation, say 2° 25' (40 mil), and subtract. This leaves a revised bearing of approximately 321° (5660 mil), for which the compass dial can be adjusted.

Placing the top right-hand edge of the compass against the landmark, pivot the whole compass until the direction of travel arrow in the base of the housing is running parallel to the eastings. Draw a line.

Find another landmark and repeat the whole procedure. For example, the second bearing is 37° (0650 mil), and approximately 35° (0610 mil) after adjustment for the magnetic variation. Draw another line as above. Your position is marked where the two lines cross.

Instruction in map and compass techniques is offered by a number of organizations, including local walking clubs, mountain rescue teams and specialized training centres. Of the latter, the addresses for Glenmore Lodge in Scotland and Plas-y-Brenin in Wales are given on page 191.

GPS (GLOBAL POSITIONING SYSTEM)

GPS provides state-of-the-art navigation – but don't forget your compass

This new and high-tech method of navigation is worthy of a mention, as in time it will replace the compass, although not entirely. Developed by the United States Department of Defense, the GPS (Global Positioning System) consists of twenty-four military satellites which orbit Earth, continually giving out the time and their position. Receiver units on Earth pick up this information. These units, known as GPS, have advanced at a phenomenal rate and, although designed primarily for the military, small hand-held units no larger than a mobile phone are available to hillwalkers. The GPS unit is able to receive and assimilate information from several satellites, converting it into a recognizable position and altitude at any point on the Earth's surface. GPS units can pinpoint your position to within 15 m (45 ft) or less.

How it Works

The GPS receiver unit searches for and then locks onto any satellite signals. The more signals it receives, the greater the accuracy, but a minimum of four is sufficient. The information received is then collated into a usable form; for example, a grid reference, height above sea level, or longitude and latitude. Individual requirements for use either on land or at sea can be programmed into the unit.

By measuring your position in relation to a number of known objects, i.e. the satellites, the receiver is able to calculate your position. This is called satellite ranging. The receiver is also able to update your position, speed and track while you are on the move and can pinpoint future waypoints, thereby removing the need for finding recognisable landmarks.

AUTHOR'S NOTE

The GPS requires tuition in its proper use, and is not a compass in the normal sense. In the UK I have found two models with good instructions: the Silver and the Garmin 40. The only way to learn either is to get out and practice. Despite its excellent qualities, the GPS system can be shut down at any time. In addition, the unit eats batteries, so don't forget your compass.

FINDING DIRECTION WITHOUT A COMPASS

Compasses may be the easiest and most convenient method of finding a direction, but what if you are without one? Many people wander off using just a map. This is fine until you get lost or bad weather disorientates you. Luckily there are a number of other methods for finding direction. All that is needed is a bit of intelligence.

STICK AND STONE METHOD

- On a sunny day find or cut a stick about 1 m long and push it upright into some level ground (**a**). The stick will cast a shadow.
- Using a small stone, mark the end of the shadow as accurately as possible (**b**).
- After fifteen to twenty minutes the shadow will have moved. Using a second small stone, mark the tip of the new shadow (**c**).
- On the earth, draw a straight line running through both stones (**d**). This is your West–East line.
- Put your left foot close to the first stone, and your right foot next to the second stone.
- You are now facing North (**e**).

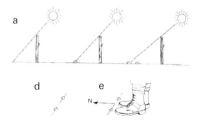

Note: The accuracy of this method depends on how level the ground is, how well the ends of the shadows are marked, and how much care is taken in placing the toes at the line. A North–South indicator can be produced if a line is drawn at right-angles to your West–East line. Any other direction can be calculated from these cardinal points.

USING A WATCH

- As Britain is in the northern hemisphere, an analogue watch can be used to establish direction.
- Check that your watch is accurately set to local time.
- Point the hour hand at the sun.
- Using a thin twig, cast a shadow along the hour hand through the central pivot.
- Cut across the angle between the hour hand and the 12 o'clock position.
- This line will be pointing due South, North being furthest from the sun.

BY NIGHT

Navigation by the stars has been used for centuries, and is still employed in map-making. Learning about the stars is beneficial in itself, but this knowledge comes into its own in survival navigation. Bright stars that seem to be grouped together in a pattern are called constellations. The shapes of these constellations and their relationship to each other don't alter. Due to the Earth's rotation, the whole of the night sky appears to revolve around one central point, and using this knowledge can help you to find directions.

Locating the Pole Star

In the northern hemisphere, a faint star called Polaris, the Pole or the North Star marks the central point. Because of its position, it always appears to be in the same place, above the North Pole. As long as Polaris can be seen, the direction of True North can be found.

To find Polaris, first locate the constellation known as The Plough or The Big Dipper. The two stars furthest from the 'handle' always point towards Polaris. Take the distance between the two stars and then follow the line straight for about six times the distance. At this point you will see Polaris.

If you are unsure which way to look or want to confirm that you have found Polaris, look for another constellation called Cassiopeia. The five stars that make up this constellation are patterned in the shape of a slightly squashed W. It is always positioned almost opposite the Plough, and Polaris can be found midway between them. As long as the sky is clear, the Plough, Cassiopeia and Polaris remain visible in the sky all night when seen from any country north of a latitude of 40°.

OBSTACLES

Many obstacles may present themselves during your walk. Some will impede your progress, while others will influence your direction of travel. Careful route selection and good map-reading can avoid most. Study your route for large rivers, steep mountains and restricted areas. Remember, obstacles to your progress do not have to be of solid matter. Getting caught out on the mountains at night will also give cause for concern.

RIVER-CROSSING

Every hillwalker will encounter a mountain stream or small river that is easy to cross by jumping over or shallow enough to safely wade through. However, at some point you will come across a large river, or one that has flooded, which you will need to cross. Of course, it is best to avoid the situation in the first place by careful route-planning and by listening to the weather forecast. Even when confronted by the obstacle, studying your map may throw up a route to follow along the waterway on foot, without encountering too much thick vegetation, to a safe crossing place (bridge or ford). If this is the case, you should take this option.

Crossing without a rope should not normally be attempted. However, if it is certain that a crossing can be safely undertaken and if the water level is relatively low, then there are certain methods by which this may be achieved. While a group offers support and stability, there may be a situation where you must cross a river alone.

AUTHOR'S NOTE

Never attempt to cross a rain-swollen river. They are deep, very fast and highly dangerous. During periods of heavy rain the flow in rivers can fluctuate rapidly. Conversely, once the rain has stopped, the water level may drop quickly. Bearing this in mind, you should decide whether it is best to wait for the water level to drop or whether it is viable to find another place to cross safely. Crossing a stream in full spate is not a decision to be taken lightly and should only be considered as an emergency procedure, a last resort when any other decision would further compromise health or safety further.

Crossing without a rope should not normally be attempted. However, if it is certain that a crossing can be safely undertaken and if the water level is relatively low, then there are certain methods by which this may be achieved. While a group offers support and stability, there may be a situation where you must cross a river alone.

CROSSING ALONE

If under normal circumstances a river crossing is deemed possible, choose the widest, slowest point, and avoid bends, as the speed of the current will increase as you wade from the inside of the bend to the outside, as will the depth of water. Wade through, rather than jumping from

Use a strong pole when crossing a river alone

stone to stone. Even a simple slip can result in an immobilizing sprain or other injury – and perhaps the loss of equipment. If possible, anyone crossing should be secured to the bank by rope or safety-line. Use a solid stick as an extra point of contact and for probing the riverbed. A walking pole for extra balance is also a good idea.

If the water is slow but deep, consider swimming across. Securing your rucksack in a tightly-tied bin-liner will form an excellent flotation aid. Weak swimmers can take off their trousers, knot the wetted leg ends, grip the waistband, then swing the trousers over their head in an arc-like motion. This will trap air in the trouser legs and provide a good flotation aid.

RIVER-CROSSING TECHNIQUES WITH A ROPE

One of the most common ways to cross a river is to secure a safety-line between the two banks. This requires the rope to be taken to the opposite bank by the first person, who should also be the strongest swimmer (1). When making his way across, by either wading or swimming, he should adopt one of the methods described above. He should also be secured to the safety-line so that he can be pulled back if he gets into difficulties. Once he is across and the line is secured, the next member (**2**) and each of the rest of the party should use a Karabiner (a metal hoop with screw-gate opening) to clip themselves onto the line before crossing. The last member should unclip the safety-line and attach it to himself before crossing, in order that he may be pulled across if necessary (**3**). If possible, weaker swimmers should have the benefit of a second line to aid and secure them. Providing there is enough rope, a similar method can be implemented using a continuous loop.

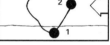

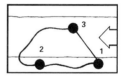

CROSSING WITHOUT A ROPE

To cross a river without a rope, three people should stand side by side, arms linked around each other's shoulders, with the weakest swimmer in the middle. Move across the river with the physically strongest member standing against the flow of the current. Move slowly, supporting each other in case one of the three should stumble or fall. Take care when entering and leaving the stream, especially if the banks are steep, hold onto the bank and help the weakest person out first.

If you flounder or slip in the water, it is important not to panic. If you are tied to a rope there will be someone there to pull you in. If you are using your rucksack as a buoyancy aid, hold on tight. Whatever happens, if you find yourself floating downstream, float feet first to fend off any obstacles and do not try to fight the current. Avoid any obstacles such as submerged branches, and if you feel the riverbed below you, try to stand.

Once you have crossed the river, you are likely to be cold, with your morale a little on the low side. Change immediately into spare dry clothing.

River-Crossing Checklist

- Plan your route to avoid having to cross water.
- Always look for a bridge or safe crossing point first.
- Cross only if absolutely necessary.
- Choose the widest and shallowest stretch.
- Never, unless in a life-threatening situation, attempt to cross a river in flood.
- If alone, use a buoyancy aid.
- Use a safety-line if one is available.

HOW TO MOVE IN THE DARK

At times it may be necessary to move in the dark, especially when a member of your party has been seriously injured and requires immediate medical attention. Of course, it is better to stay put, but if moving in darkness is the only option in your situation, you need to know the safest ways of doing this.

Move only as far as you need to get out of immediate danger or to make contact, and then sit tight. To venture further when it is not necessary is to risk more injury. Although being in complete darkness can be frightening, stay calm and take stock of the situation. Check that you have no other source of lighting on you. If you are moving with other people make sure that everyone stays in touching distance with the next person. If you have a rope or lifeline, rope everyone together.

Unless a life really depends on it, do not try crossing a river in darkness – it is extremely dangerous. However, if you must, use one of the techniques described in the section on River-crossing (see page 76). While it is a good idea to follow a stream or river on the flat, never follow water down a steep mountainside, as it will inevitably have a waterfall somewhere. Even if the waterfall is small, it will be enough to cause injuries if you fall over it in the dark.

You may find that your senses become heightened in the dark. This is good, as you can use them to your advantage. However, be aware that heightened senses mean even familiar noises may sound much louder and closer, which to some people can be unnerving – stay calm, and talk to yourself or each other if necessary.

AUTHOR'S NOTE

When I first joined the army I was told by one of the instructors that if I kept my mouth open during darkness it would increase my sound reception. Whether this is true or not I have always done it, and find that it does work. Likewise, during the many night operations I carried out during my SAS years, whenever danger was imminent the senses reached out into the darkness and often tingled the brain with a warning. Over the years I have learnt to accept this and become cautious when these danger signals arise. Do not be afraid of the dark – animals will normally avoid you, and another human prowling around will most probably be equally unsure.

USING THE SENSES

The only way to achieve 'night vision' is by waiting until the eyes have become accustomed to the darkness, and then maintaining it by shutting out any bright light source such as a torch or a car headlight. If you must look at a bright light once you have your night vision, always cover one eye to protect it. Remember though, that low light conditions can cause the eye to be deceived, especially by distance. It is vital to use all the senses when walking at night.

MEMORY

Prior to darkness falling, you should have a good idea of the 'look' of the surrounding countryside. If your memory is good, it may aid you in finding a route out in the dark. Distance can be confusing, as you will be forced to move more slowly. Try, if possible, to locate features which can be easily identified. If you have no idea of your exact location, always move cautiously downhillas this is more likely to lead you to the safety of a road or track.

Touch

Touch is particularly good when it is totally dark or when you are moving over steep and rocky ground. Again, always move downhill, using your hands as if you were a climber, keeping three points in contact with the rock at all times. Use your hands and arms to make sure that the immediate space before you is clear of any obstacles and is secure to step on. If the ground is uneven or there is the possibility of a dangerous drop, crawl on your hands and knees.

Light and Sound

Being caught out on a mountain during the hours of darkness does have two great advantages – those of light and sound. I know of few places in the British Isles where one can stand and not see the distant glow of a major city or the light of a small house. They may be some way off but they are still your beacon to safety. Sound can also help: metal banging on metal, the rhythmic flow of water and the noise of domestic animals all echo through the night and, if interpreted correctly, will help guide you to safety. Likewise, the sound of thunder will warn you of a coming storm, but the lightning will also illuminate the area for you, although somewhat briefly. When moving on lower ground, you will hear a river or fast-flowing stream long before you fall into it, but if you think there may be a steep drop or riverbank ahead, try throwing a stone and listen for the sound of it hitting earth or water. The sound of a search party will also carry to you, and you should always be alert to their efforts.

Walking in a forest at night generally means there is little or no light. Try putting your arms out in front of you and tilting your head back to look up at the treetops. You will find there is a contrast between the dark forest and the lighter sky, a contrast that will help guide you through the forest. If you are lucky enough to come across a forest track, the same method will keep you on course. As there are no trees on the track, there will be a clean edge to the treetop silhouette.

When walking over snow-covered ground on a clear night, the starlight and moonlight will reflect off the white surface. However, should it start snowing hard or if the wind is blowing a gale, you should reconsider your night movement, as progress in a blizzard is life-threatening: moving in a blizzard has a disorienting effect and pitfalls below the surface are obscured.

However, on a clear moonlit night it is possible to see for up to 100 m and you should be able to look up and identify the various star constellations. The Pole Star will give you an approximate northerly direction and thus all other points of the compass can be worked out (see page 75).

Camping Out

If you intend to camp out during your walks, you will need to consider where you are going to sleep and, more importantly, how you are going to protect yourself against the elements. In the more popular walking areas such as the Lake District, Peak District or Brecon Beacons you can always find a wide variety of homes and farms offering bed and breakfast. However, if you prefer the isolation of the mountains or the tranquillity of the valleys, you may prefer to camp out or use a bothy.

BARNS AND BOTHIES

Bothies, mountain huts, barns and derelicts are little more than old discarded country dwellings which provide a ready-made shelter for the hillwalker in remote areas. In many areas they have been renovated to the point where they will keep the wind and rain out, and a few are provided with fuel and a fireplace. To the weary hillwalker they provide simple accommodation (in most cases free) but you are expected to provide your own sleeping equipment and cook your own food. If you do use such a building, remember those that come after you, and leave the place as tidy as you found it. Do not be tempted (unless it is an emergency) to use buildings intended for animal use, as they will contain droppings and will be crawling with lice and ticks. Contact the Mountain Bothies Association (see page 191) for details of bothies in the United Kingdom.

CAMP SITES

The more traditional way of camping out is to use a tent, either pitched in a recognized camp site or in a permitted area. If you are not sure where to camp, it is always best to ask the local landowner for permission. Most appreciate the gesture and will indicate a good spot. Pitch your tent carefully, with the tail/back end facing into the wind. Select your site carefully – for example, away from damp ground or too close to a river. Mist will collect over the water during the early morning and your tent will get very damp if you are too close. If you find yourself on wet ground or think that it will rain in the night, pitch your tent on a small mound where the ground will carry excess water away. Don't be tempted to dig drainage ditches around your tent. The site owner or farmer will not appreciate it, and in most cases a ditch will merely hold the water around your tent.

After a while, camping in the same spot can have an impact on the ground. Moving your tent every two to

three days will avoid damage to the underlying vegetation. Clear the camp site of litter before leaving.

CHOOSING A TENT

Even if you have not planned on camping out, there are other reasons for carrying a small tent. The weather may suddenly turn nasty, forcing you to seek shelter, or a member of your party may be taken ill and require the protection of a tent. Tents keep out the wind and rain, while keeping the warmth in. In an emergency most modern tents can be erected in a matter of minutes.

You will find a wide variety of tents available, ranging from a few pounds to several hundred, the price reflecting the quality and style of tent and its intended usage. There are tunnel tents, hooped tents, dome tents, ridge tents, and so on; as a hillwalker you should choose a tent to suit your needs. Consider what sort of weather you are likely to be camping out in. For British conditions you will require a fully weatherproof tent with some form of porch in which you can cook and store your rucksack. When choosing a tent you should ask yourself certain questions and always buy the best quality tent within your budget. Most tents are supplied with a stuff sack, which will house the lightweight flexible poles, tent and flysheet if separate.

Cotton tents do not suffer from condensation problems but are prone to getting wet, which makes them hard to dry and heavier to carry. All nylon tents are lighter and fully waterproof but suffer badly with condensation. A good compromise is to choose a cotton tent with a waterproof groundsheet and a nylon waterproof outer. Gore-Tex tents are another option, as they are light and breathable, but very expensive. Tents can be costly so always make sure that when you return home your tent is put out to dry, as this will prevent it becoming mildewed and rotten.

Choose your tent with care, and always take into account the following:

- How large should it be, and will you be sharing it with someone else on a permanent basis? Sharing cuts down weight, especially if the tent comes in separate parts.

- Weight. Ideally your tent, complete with outer flysheet, should not exceed 4 kg (9 lb) for two people, and half that if you camp alone.

- Insects can be a real problem, so make sure the tent entrance has a well-fitted insect screen.

- Consider where you will be camping. Dome tents with a large inner volume may not be very stable when positioned on a high windy plateau.

- Tents can be very bland in colour. Don't forget that your tent may have to be used in an emergency, so despite what the conservationists say, choose a bright colour.

- If you want serious lightweight camping you might try a bivvy bag.

AUTHOR'S NOTE

During my years in the SAS I used a one-man hooped bivvy bag, which I found to be adequate for a one-night stop in the countryside. It protected me against some really vicious weather, was comfortable, dry and could be erected in minutes. If it had any drawback it was the amount of space it offered. That said, it weighed in at less than 1 kg (2.2 lb).

CARBON MONOXIDE POISONING

Carbon monoxide poisoning can easily occur if you burn a fire or a stove in an unventilated place, such as a tent. The gas is colourless and odourless – once you realise that you are being poisoned, you may lack the energy to escape. It is best to be aware of the dangers and make sure that you have adequate ventilation, and that the flame on your stove burns blue instead of yellow. The symptoms are headache, lethargy, confusion, nausea and vomiting, followed by distressed breathing and loss of consciousness. Get the casualty into the fresh air as quickly as possible. Put out the offending stove or fire and ventilate the tent.

UNEXPECTED OVERNIGHT CAMP

An unexpected incident can occur at any time and may well make it necessary for you to spend a night outdoors. Providing no one is injured, and there is no real emergency, such a situation will test all your skills of improvisation and add to your hillwalking experience. In reality you should have about your person some form of minimal survival kit (see page 176). However, you may have only what you stand up in. If you are alone you must formulate your own actions, but if you are in a group you must rely on the judgment of the party leader or senior. The leader of any hillwalking party should have enough experience to improvise a basic shelter from the materials in the area. Just as importantly, he should be able to keep the hopes of the party high, but realistic. The chances of survival for a party that has given up hope will be a lot less than those with a sense of optimism.

EMERGENCY SHELTERS

If you find yourself in a survival situation – a situation in which something unexpected has happened or your safety is put in jeopardy – you should decide on the order of priorities, and where the need for shelter lies within that order. For hillwalkers, the need for shelter will come from an injury or the need for protection

A simple shelter sheet will provide protection from the rain but not the wind

against the weather. The most dangerous conditions include cold, wind, rain and snow. It is essential to protect yourself against these, as each of them is a factor which hastens hypothermia. Exposure to any combination of these can produce fatal results long before any shortage of food or water will take effect.

Even in summery conditions or hot climates, shelter from the sun is needed so as to avoid overheating of the body. It may not affect the survivor as rapidly as loss of body heat, but it can still be deadly, as it will very quickly lead to a loss of body fluids.

CHOOSING A SITE

Caught without a tent or emergency survival bag, temporary shelter is quickest found among the natural features surrounding you. Seek it in or around trees, thick bushes or natural hollows. If they are safe, make use of caves, rock overhangs or any available natural shelter. Never waste time and energy constructing a temporary shelter or windbreak if nature or circumstance already provide it. Choose the best site that gives natural cover from the wind. If no such cover is

Adapting natural shelter should be your first choice of providing protection

available, consider making a windbreak. If you are likely to be in the position for some time, construct a shelter as near as possible to sources of building materials and, very importantly, firewood. Any spot in a forest and near a fast-flowing stream can be the site for a good temporary camp.

WARNING

If you are forced to camp in lowlands during heavy rain, you should recognize the danger of floods. On the coast also keep the tides in mind. In mountainous areas make sure that the chosen site is not in the path of possible avalanches or rockfalls. If you are in the forest, look around for fallen trees which may indicate that it is an area of shallow soil. If the wind can blow one tree over, it could do the same to others nearby.

EMERGENCY BUILDING MATERIALS

- **Sheeting.** Any type of sheeting can be utilised for shelter; groundsheets, plastic sheeting, sacks, canvas or blankets.

- **Turf.** Turf can be used for construction on very flat open areas where trees and shrubs are scarce. In many countries it is used as a roofing material. If you don't have a knife for cutting turf, a flat, sharp-edged stone may well suffice.

- **Foliage.** With foliage it is possible to construct an excellent long-lasting waterproof shelter. Where available, use large-leafed foliage.

- **Rocks and Stones.** Where the ground is hard or foliage is in very short supply it will be possible to make a good shelter out of rocks and stones.

- **Snow.** If you are caught out in wintry conditions, and the depth allows it, snow can be a good source of building material.

FORMS OF QUICK SHELTER

LEAN-TO FRAME

The lean-to frame is the standard shelter pattern, probably because it is one of the simplest. When setting up the frame, make sure that the roof slopes down into the prevailing wind. The covering can be almost anything, from foliage to plastic sacks or a groundsheet – even turf blocks can be used. A firm mud or turf layer on top of foliage will harden, preventing the shelter cover from being blown away and making it more wind- and waterproof. The sides of the shelter can be filled in using a similar foliage-and-mud method or could be walled with turf blocks.

TREE BIVOUAC

A small shelter can be made quite quickly using any small tree. Cut part way through the trunk at a point about shoulder-height until you are able to push the upper portion over so that its top rests on the ground.

The stem should be left attached to the butt. Cut away the branches on the underside and break the upstanding branches on the outside so that they hang down. Thatch the shelter using the foliage cut from below.

THE SNOW TRENCH

A hole in the snow provides temporary shelter as an emergency measure, and it can be improved to make a simple shelter for one man. If the snow is soft, branches or sheeting of some kind will be needed for the roof.

THE FIR TREE SNOW SHELTER

If you are in a wooded area, by far the simplest shelter can be found under a large fir tree. There will often be a natural hollow in the snow around the base of the tree trunk to give you a good start. Dig away the snow from the base, using it to build up and improve the protection on either side of the shelter area. Cut away the low branches on the side to use either as bedding or to interweave with the branches on your side to improve the overhead cover. You can build a fire under the tree, but make sure it is at least part of the way around the trunk from your shelter. This is because the heat will

In winter the base of a large fir tree provides not only shelter, but also bedding and fuel

melt the snow in the branches above the fire. This type of shelter can be readily made in forests during summer (even when there is no snow) and winter. The foundation provided by nature needs only slight improvement to make it warm and comfortable.

THE SNOW CAVE

This type of shelter requires a depth of snow of 2 m (6 ft) or more. The simplest approach would be to build into a snow drift or cornice. To improve the snow cave, aim for as many of the features shown in the cross-section as you can. Sometimes this type of shelter is more difficult to make than it appears, because of the hardness of the packed snow. Without some tools it may be impossible. Make sure that the inside roof is always dome shaped, or you will wake up in the morning with it on your head.

Snow is an adaptable material from which many types of shelter can be made

SLEEPING BAGS

We spend a third of our day sleeping, and even more when camping out, as we go to bed earlier and normally want to remain in our cosy bag just a little bit longer. For this reason it is worthwhile choosing a good-quality sleeping bag. There are many different types on the market and there are only two real elements to look for – warmth and construction. Weight is also important, but for the average hillwalker many of the sleeping bags you look at will be of very similar weights.

A good sleeping bag will provide warmth and a comfortable night's sleep

Warmth is the most important factor and the argument over which is the best filling, duck down or synthetic, still goes on. The answer is neither, as it is the air trapped inside the insulation and not the material that keeps you warm. In very general terms, the more loft (thickness) a sleeping bag has the warmer it will be. Synthetic is cheaper and has the advantage of not losing its insulation properties when wet. Down, on the other hand, is lighter and can be compressed into a much smaller space, but collapses when wet.

The construction of the sleeping bag is also important. Cheap oblong bags with a wraparound zip are little more than a folded blanket. A mummy-shaped bag is warmer simply because there is less space for your body to heat. You should also choose a sleeping bag that has a hood, as 80 per cent of your body heat escapes from your head. Likewise, a sleeping bag with a boxed foot section will help you feel comfortable and unrestricted.

When buying a new sleeping bag, check the following points:

- The sleeping bag should not be too large.
- It should have a draught strip behind the zip to protect against warm air leakage.
- It should have a hood and a foot box.
- The zip should be operable from both inside and out.
- The filling should be appropriate to your needs.
- The stitching should be of a high quality.

AUTHOR'S NOTE

If your build is short and you find that your sleeping bag is too large, try shortening the bag by sealing off the bottom with a waist belt or tying a piece of cord around it. This helps cut down the amount of wasted space around your feet, thus increasing the temperature and heat retention inside the sleeping bag.

SURVIVAL BAGS AND INSULATION MATS

Every hillwalker is advised to carry at least one survival bag as part of a survival kit, or in the flap of a rucksack. Survival bags are invaluable as they can provide shelter from both wind and rain. They come in a variety of sizes, colours and thicknesses, but all serve the same basic purpose.

A Camo-Glo is two large, strong polythene bags, one of which is placed inside the other and the cavity filled with dry straw, leaves or grass, to form an emergency insulated bag. A good survival bag will act as a sleeping bag or can be converted into a simple tent. Some survival bags even have emergency instructions printed on the front.

A survival bag will be uncomfortable but it will help protect you against the elements

Insulation mats have been around for many years and they provide much-needed protection from ground that's cold and damp. Most modern sleeping mats are made from specially-laminated EVA closed-cell foam. They vary little in size, normally being about 20 cm (8 in) wide and 60 cm (2 ft) long, and come either rolled or folded. Insulation mats are extremely lightweight, cost very little money and are excellent value.

COOKERS

There was a time when all the camper needed was a small camp fire. This would provide heat for cooking, light and a modicum of comfort. However, in addition to leaving a permanent scar on the earth, open fires, especially in summer, pose a huge risk to forests and dry grassland. Moreover, modern camping cookers are convenient, as they do not need a continuous supply of dead wood, are simple to light and control, and, although it is not recommended, they can be used indoors.

There are two types of cooker, solid fuel and liquid fuel, the main difference being regulation and control of the heat source. Solid-fuel cookers have been around for over two thousand years in one form or another and they are simply a brick-type block of fuel that burns in a container and acts as a cooker. Modern-day variations use a small tablet, usually constructed of Hexamine, placed on a small folding metal cooker on top of which a pot is balanced. With a little practice, solid-fuel blocks are simple to light. However, they do need protection against the wind. The solid-fuel cooker has the drawback of allowing the flame to penetrate through to the ground, so consideration should be given to the placing of your cooker in order to prevent forest fires.

Liquid-fuel cookers fall into two main categories, gas- and petroleum-based mixtures, the difference being the burning time and pressurization. Petrol- and kerosene-type cookers normally require pressurization and they have a much shorter burning duration when compared to the weight of gas cooker fuel. Gas cookers such as propane and butane do not require pressurization, are lighter and have a longer burning time. They also have fewer moving parts which makes maintenance much easier. Both types are produced in a range of sizes, and are convenient to light and use. Fuel for petroleum-based mixtures is readily available worldwide, whereas the small individual gas containers and solid-fuel cookers are generally restricted to camping outlets.

COOKER SAFETY

If used carefully and the manufacturer's recommendations are adhered too, all forms of camping cooker are relatively safe. Fuel spillage, over-pressurization and fuel canisters not fitted properly are the main causes of flare-ups and dangerous mishaps. Badly-placed cookers and unbalanced cooking pots also present problems resulting in scalding and burns. It is for this reason that camping cookers should not be used in a tent or confined spaces. Many people construct a reflective shield in windy conditions. Providing this is done properly there is no problem. However, using a shield constructed of flammable material, or placing the shield too close to the cooker, can cause overheating. If you are using a shield and your cooker is fitted with a pressure release valve, make sure it is pointing away from those doing the cooking.

Gas cookers require the removal and replacement of gas-filled cartridges. In the main this is extremely safe but you should do it in the open and away from any naked flame. New cartridges should not be exposed to heat or left in direct sunlight, and old cartridges should be disposed of in a responsible manner.

IMPROVISED COOKERS

If you find yourself without a cooker or you are in a survival situation, it is not too difficult to improvise one. For a heat-source required for a short period of time you are best building a small fire surrounded by a ring of stones to prevent it spreading. Cooking on an open fire is not easy, as the food has a tendency to burn on the outside and be uncooked on the inside. A simple improvement is to construct a basic stove.

BILLYCAN COOKER

At the height of the American Depression, almost every unemployed person roaming the country looking for

work carried some form of improvised cooker constructed from a large metal can. The size of the can is fairly immaterial but a large catering-sized bean can is about right. Using any available metal can or box, it is a simple matter of punching a few holes in the base and around the bottom of the tin. This will provide the air required to make the fire burn. Other small improvements can be made by cutting down the lip a few inches and bending the metal inwards to form a stand on which you can rest your cooking pot. This type of cooker is economical as far as fuel is concerned (anything nontoxic that will burn can be used), and is well-suited to colder conditions, since, with care, it could be used inside a shelter (not a tent). Additionally, the billycan cooker may be carried once it has cooled down.

YUKON STOVE

The Yukon stove is a simple and safe way of building a fire and utilizing its heat. If you are in one location for more than twenty-four hours, and the ground and regulations allow it, you should certainly seriously consider building this type of stove. The Yukon stove normally takes about two hours for one person to construct, providing most of the materials are to hand. It requires only rocks, stones and mud for its construction, fashioning a hollow tortoiseshell hump as the basic design. At one side you must leave a hole for the intake of fuel and air, with another at the top to act as a chimney. Two further refinements are very desirable. The first is the building in of a metal box or large can into the back wall. This will provide an excellent oven. You must remember, however, that food placed in the oven will be burned unless it is separated from the metal by small sticks or stones. If twigs are used they will turn into charcoal after a day or two. You should keep this for use in deodorizing boiled water if necessary, and for other medicinal purposes. The second improvement is to use a large flat rock as part of the top of the stove, which can be used as a griddle for frying bacon and eggs.

One of the Yukon's major advantages is that it can be left unattended while you are working at other activities. Wet clothing can be laid over the outside of the stove and will dry without burning. You can also warm yourself without risk of being burnt.

FIRE-LIGHTING

Fire is one of the essential aids to survival, and the ability to light a fire in difficult circumstances is a survival technique of inestimable value. The discovery of fire was one of humanity's great advances, since with the

provision of shelter, it allowed man to modify his environment, enabling him to survive in otherwise unsuitable climatic conditions.

It is because fire has been such a vital part of man's history that it also plays an important psychological role in survival efforts, as it is a great source of comfort. The lighting of a fire is proof that a survivor can control some, at least, of the dangers which face him. It also provides a sense of achievement in that the survivor has replaced, in his emergency situation, one of the major elements which contribute to normal life. Even more important, of course, are the varying practical uses of fire. Fire will provide heat and light, together with the ability to cook food, purify water and sterilize medical equipment. Clothing can be dried, and signals can be generated, thus seeking help. Fire is a powerful tool.

CARE WITH FIRES

Only light a fire where necessary, for, although a camp fire can be enjoyable, out of control it can also cause great damage to the local environment. Make sure that you locate such a fire in a position where it cannot do much damage, such as in a dry stream bed, although be careful about using certain rocks, such as limestone, as when heated these have a tendency to explode. Collect only dead wood for fuel. Never cut live wood, but bear in mind that even dead wood has an important role in the natural cycle of regeneration. Therefore, only take as much as you need for a small fire. When leaving the site, ensure that the fire is completely out and the ashes cold, replace any rocks used and try to eradicate as many traces of the fire as possible.

THE BASIC ELEMENTS

Any fire requires three elements: heat, fuel and oxygen. If any one element is missing, a fire will not burn.

When considering the supply of fuel, it is helpful to recall that fire is a form of chain reaction. Part of the heat generated by the combustion of any fuel is required to ignite the succeeding supply. The initial supply of heat available to start the fire is usually small – a match flame or spark which lasts only a few seconds. It follows that the starting fuel, which must be set alight by such a brief flame, must be a material that ignites very easily. This form of fuel is referred to as tinder. Tinder must be dry, so that it will ignite readily. It is therefore essential that, before attempting to set light to the tinder, you make certain that there is a supply of kindling ready to hand.

Kindling will consist of small dry twigs, followed by dry sticks, which will enable a small, hot fire to be built. You may then gradually add larger sticks until you have a fire which will burn long enough to ignite small logs. When such a fire has been established, even green logs can be added, since the heat available will boil out the sap long before the logs burn. At first, however, the wood you gather should be dead, and as dry as possible.

Before you attempt to light your fire, it is essential to collect, grade and stack the fuel into tinder, kindling and heavy fuel. Be sure to gather sufficient quantities to build and establish your fire. It is also very important not to fall into the common error of piling kindling and other wood onto the fire too soon. Doing so will probably limit the supply of oxygen and the fire will die. If you ensure that the fire is well ventilated, it will burn efficiently, and the smaller wood will produce less smoke.

HEAT

The heat required to start a fire can be generated in a number of ways. The easiest to use is an open flame, from a match or lighter. Sparks from flint and steel, or from an electrical source, can be used to ignite tinder. A magnifying glass or parabolic reflector, in sunny conditions, can do the same. Friction is a good source of heat, but it is the least preferable of these methods owing to the amount of effort and time involved. Details of the various heat-sources are given later in the section.

LIGHTING A FIRE

It is well worthwhile taking some care when choosing a site for your fire. If you have, or are going to build, a shelter, you will not want it to be filled with smoke. On the other hand, heat from the fire should be available within the cover.

Points to remember when building a fire:

- Choose and prepare the site for your fire.
- Check the wind direction, and the dryness of the location.
- Look at the availability of fuel in the area.
- Gather your fuel supply and sort it into categories.
- Prepare the tinder.
- Light and build the fire – slowly. Do not smother it.
- Provide the fire with good ventilation once it is started.
- If conditions are windy, some form of shield must be erected or provided before attempting to light your fire.

Once the fire is established, it is often useful to enclose it in a circle of stones, if they are readily available. This will define the size of the fire and lessen the danger of it spreading. If larger stones are used on the windward side, the fire will be able to burn more steadily than if it were entirely open to the wind. This is important, because a continually fanned fire consumes much more fuel than one that is sheltered. Gathering wood for a roaring fire can use up a great deal of time and energy.

A fire may appear to have burned out overnight. If so, check the ashes and embers, as they will often retain enough heat for you to be able to relight your fire from them. If the ashbed feels warm, gently push some tinder down into the ashes. Use a twig to do this or a burned finger could be the result! Once the tinder starts smoking, gently blow or fan into flames, and add tinder as required to relight the fire. Always keep a good supply of fuel to hand, and perhaps an adequate amount of earth, sand or water to control the flames if necessary.

SOURCES OF TINDER

- Decayed or powdered dry wood
- Pulverized outer bark (cypress, cedar, birch)
- Crushed cones from evergreen trees
- Any old nest material (rat's, bird's, etc.)
- Scorched or charred cloth, especially linen
- Cotton wool (best covered in charcoal)
- Some photographic film
- Charred rope, lint from twine, canvas, bandages, etc.
- Petrol or cooker fuel
- Insect repellent
- Oil

The last three should be used in conjunction with some solid form of tinder, or poured over sand or absorbent material. All tinder obtained from solids is most effective if it is reduced to shreds, threads or fibres and loosely piled to ensure good ventilation with enhanced combustibility.

HEAT-SOURCES

Heat can be obtained from many sources, and in cold climates the ability to produce a flame is absolutely essential for survival.

MATCHES

All hillwalkers should carry a supply of matches as a matter of course on all outdoor trips, for they are the easiest and most obvious means of generating flame. They are, however, vulnerable to the effects of damp. Matches can be protected from water by dipping each separate match into molten wax, covering the head and half the stick. Spraying it with hair lacquer can protect the outside of the box.

Special wind- and waterproof matches can be purchased from most camping outlets. These are not expensive and will

Wind- and waterproof matches are purposely designed for survival

provide a constant flame for about six seconds in the worst weather. Always aim for **One Match, One Fire**.

LIGHTERS

A lighter can be a lifesaver. It does not suffer the effects of damp and will generally light over two hundred fires. Even when the lighter fuel is eventually exhausted, don't forget that sparks from the flint can be used, with tinder, to light a fire.

CANDLES

A candle, however small, will prolong the active life of your matches or lighter, besides helping you light the fire. This is because most people can light a candle with one match or first time with a lighter. You then have a constant naked flame to ignite the tinder, even if it is slightly damp.

Even when tinder is damp, it is possible to light a fire using a candle

To put this technique to use, cut a small hole in the ground or build a small shield of stones around the candle. Pile the tinder over the hole or shield, and slide the lighted candle underneath. As soon as the tinder starts burning, remove the candle. This is a particularly good method of lighting a fire if it is raining or the fuel is wet.

FLINT AND STEEL

This is one of the cheapest and better items on the market. Developed for the military, it consists of a 5 cm (2 in) flint which is stroked by a serrated hacksaw blade, producing a large amount of sparks. Properly used, a flint and steel will light up to two thousand fires, irrespective of being wet or dry.

A flint and steel is good for lighting over 2000 fires

A similar product is an aluminium block impregnated with magnesium housing the flint along one of its edges.

The sharp edge of the hacksaw blade will first produce shavings from the block. These can then be ignited with sparks struck from the flint. The heat produced is brief but the heat output of burning magnesium is in excess of 2700 °C (5000 °F). This item of firelighting equipment is highly recommended for inclusion in any survival kit.

RUBBISH DISPOSAL

Most hillwalkers understand the value of the countryside and never drop litter. However, one does not have far to walk into the mountains before some form of can or wrapper can be found. Some rubbish can be burned in your camp site, while nontoxic liquid may be disposed of in an open pit well away from any water supply. Be very careful how you dispose of plastic bags and polythene as they are particularly lethal to animals. The best advice is to take your rubbish home and dispose of it in a proper refuse bin.

Food

Eating in the outdoors is a pleasure akin to the hillwalking itself. There is little better than stopping for a cup of tea and a sandwich at lunchtime while overlooking some magnificent scenery.

However, it is not just a matter of eating – it's also a matter of what we eat. Hillwalking is an arduous exercise with an average usage of around 3500-4500 calories per six-hour walking day. The body derives its energy from what is eaten, and stores energy in the form of fat and carbohydrates. Fats release their energy slowly and only when the carbohydrates have remained low for a period of time, i.e. when an activity is burning more calories than the body is consuming. The carbohydrates, which are stored as glycogen in the muscle, provide the energy to meet the immediate demands placed on the body through vigorous exercise. As the glycogen is depleted the body becomes exhausted and the need arises to rest and replenish our energy by eating food.

Any hillwalker is best advised to eat a normal diet but one which is rich in carbohydrates, with average protein levels and low fat. This can be achieved by purchasing fresh food and making your own menus, or subscribing to ready-made camping meals. There are many points for and against: tinned food is heavy; fresh food is healthy but has a fixed shelf-life; freeze-dried food is light and needs reconstituting. How you eat and what food you eat

will depend on whether you intend to camp out or return
to your accommodation each night.

In accommodation where breakfast and an evening meal
are provided, a simple bag of sandwiches and fruit,
together with a flask of hot drink, is sufficient. However,
you should not forget to carry at least one extra day's
food to carry you through any survival situation. This
pack should not be pilfered to supplement your day's
food.

The range of outdoor camping food is vast and comes in
a variety of forms. Your choice should be made taking
into account the length of stay outdoors and the
difficulty of the walk, with the main emphasis being
placed on weight. It is a good idea to balance out any
tinned or packet food with a supplement of items such as
bread, and fresh vegetables such as onions, tomatoes, etc.
(only take fresh food that can be eaten raw or after a
small amount of cooking). Fresh eggs can be carried for
breakfast. Break them into a large-necked polythene
bottle with a good screw top. This way you can pour one
or two eggs into a pan for cooking. They will last a
maximum of three days.

WET PACKS

These contain normal cooked food as one would find in
a tin, but packed in a foil pouch or tray. Their only
advantage over cans is the packaging. You will still be
required to carry the water weight held within the food,
as the difference in weight between a can and the foil
pack is minimal. Some wet-pack foods can be cooked in

their transit containers. However, it is best to put the contents into a proper cooking pot to avoid burning the bottom.

Freeze-dried Food

This type of food has improved dramatically over the past few years and is ideal for camping due to its light weight. The packs contain 96 per cent real food, as opposed to 80 per cent water in wet foods. They are normally packed in a foil pouch which enables boiling water to be added, thus reconstituting the contents hot in the bag. The food can also be cooked normally on a heat-source and by adding water. Menus include breakfasts, main meals and desserts, and an excellent vegetarian choice is available. Meals take about five minutes when cooked in the pack and about seven minutes when cooked conventionally. Freeze-dried food has a shelf-life of up to three years.

HEATER MEALS

These are pre-cooked food that is packed in a plastic tray and foil-sealed. The meal comes with a water-activated heater unit complete with a small sachet of water, fork, napkin and salt and pepper. The meal takes about fourteen minutes for it to become hot. Heater meals have a shelf-life of one and a half to two years.

HOT CANS

These are cans of food which can be cooked without the need for fuel. This is done by puncturing a water-activated membrane surrounding the inner can in a similar way to the heater meals. They are, however, very heavy, with a food weight of 425 g (15 oz), and an overall weight of 870 g (30 oz). They have a calorific value of around 360, with a cooking time of between twelve and fifteen minutes.

RATION PACKS

You may wish to choose a ration pack, which contains all your daily food requirements. Most are based on long-term research and give a tasty, nutritious and well-balanced diet. Most ration packs are especially enriched with high protein, mineral and calorie content, designed to provide a high proportion of complex carbohydrates, which provide the body with a form of fuel easily converted into energy.

A pre-made ration pack ensures three good meals a day

Ration packs come in lightweight variations for those intending to stay away from civilization for a long time, and also in normal one-, two- and three-day packs. In addition to the main meals, ration packs contain all other sundries needed for eating and cooking outdoors.

SURVIVAL RATIONS

Survival rations are designed to keep you alive and supply you with energy. There are some which are no more than a vitaminized biscuit made from compressed ingredients. You don't want to know about these! They are intended for real long-term survival and should not be purchased for hillwalking. A better option is to buy a purpose-made survival ration which has the benefit of having been fully tested over a period of years.

SURVIVAL FOOD

As a hillwalker you are in the mountains to enjoy yourself and not to ravage the countryside. There are many books on survival, all of which demonstrate how to forage for food by putting down traps and picking wild plants. **Don't do it.** If you have prepared

Always carry a survival ration and be ready for the unexpected

properly, you should have sufficient food and water to last you for at least two days. Even if you have nothing with you, the body can last up to four days without water and four weeks without any food, so there is no justification for using survival food techniques within the British Isles, other than using a survival ration.

Water

Nothing is more important to your survival than your water supply. The human body – itself about 90 per cent water – cannot maintain its efficiency without a regular minimum intake. The amount required varies according to climate and the level of activity being carried out. Even in a temperate climate the daily requirement is 2.5 litres (4.5 pints). If your efficiency is to be maintained, this requirement has to be met. In addition, everything possible must be done to make certain that the water is pure. Water procurement involves two factors: quality and quantity.

By and large, tapwater is safe enough, as is the water drawn from small streams in uninhabited mountainous areas (although purification is advised for any outdoor water source). It is essential to remember that much surface water, especially if stagnant or muddy, will be contaminated with waterborne diseases and will be extremely dangerous to drink unless purified. Do not underestimate this risk. The disease-inducing and other harmful organisms contained in impure water constitute one of the greatest enemies of survival. If your only source of water is impure – or even suspect – do not drink any until it has been filtered and purified.

WATER HAZARDS

Many diseases are caught through drinking contaminated water. These include dysentery, cholera, typhoid and hepatitis A. Water that is contaminated by sewage puts the hillwalker at a very high risk. Even washing in water can be dangerous, as some waterborne molluscs are infested with parasites.

Follow these basic safety rules when drinking water:

- Never drink from any source unless you are certain it is safe. This includes outside taps.
- Never drink directly from lakes, rivers, streams, etc.
- Boiled water is the safest form of drinking water. Boil for at least five minutes.
- Filter and purify all drinking water not from a safe, recognizable source.

WATER CARRIERS

How much water to carry will depend on the route, and previous experience in the area. Water is heavy, so carry no more than 2 litres (3.5 pints) for a normal walking day where you have breakfasted and dined in accommodation. Where you intend to camp out overnight, replenish your water as close as possible to your camp site.

There are numerous types of water bottles on the market. For walking, choose one that holds at least 1 litre (2 pints) of water and which will fit neatly into the side pocket of your rucksack. Always check that the top has a good screw-on cap with a waterproof seal. For your base camp you will need a larger container which can be filled locally. This should have a capacity of at least 2 gallons (9 litres).

FILTERING

Recent years have seen the emergence of a range of new (albeit somewhat expensive) water filters which should satisfy the hillwalker's needs. In general, these have a ceramic filter which removes all suspended matter and pathogens, including *e.coli*, cryptosporidium, cholera and amoebae. In most models the filter can be replaced to extend the active life. The units work by placing a tube from the bottom end of the pump into the water and operating a hand pump. A second tube at the top end allows clean water to be collected. Depending on the type you buy, the flow rate to produce 1 litre

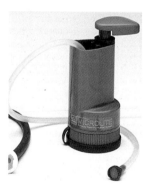

Modern water filters are extremely efficient and will cope with most types of bacteria

(2 pints) can vary from one to ten minutes.

It is also worth mentioning that there is now a compact filter which not only removes contamination but also converts seawater into fresh water. This is the smallest hand-operated desalinator in the world, filtering out some 98 per cent of the sea salt.

PURIFICATION

The best way to purify water is to treat it with purification tablets, which are available from most chemists and camping outlets. If you prefer you can use effective iodine crystals instead of the tablets. Both crystals and tablets will make contaminated water drinkable in about fifteen minutes. The amount of tablets or crystals needed will depend on the type you buy; follow the manufacturer's instructions and never be tempted to add extra as this may cause a build-up of iodine in the body. Remember tablets and crystals only kill the bacteria – they do not filter particles.

There is one ingenious device called the water-purifying straw, with which you can suck water directly into your mouth from any source. As the water passes through the straw a remarkable 96 per cent of bacteria and viruses are killed. The straw has a capacity of some 40 litre (70 pints) before the filter becomes waterclogged and ineffective.

SURVIVAL FILTERING AND PURIFICATION

You should always choose your water from the freshest source available, the best way being to collect rainwater on a clean plastic sheet. If you cannot do this, a fast-running stream should be used (larger rivers are prone to pollutants from sewage and factories).

The first step towards making water fit to drink is filtration. This will remove any creatures of any size, as well as mud particles, leaves or other foreign matter. Clean sand held in a short sleeve, sock or cloth can be used effectively.

If no purification tablets are available, boil the water for five minutes. Heat the water sufficiently to agitate the water, thereby ensuring equal distribution of heat. If you are using snow, remember you will use a great deal of fuel to produce a small amount of water. Charcoal bits from your fire, crushed and added an hour before drinking to any purified water, will help remove unpleasant tastes or smells. Don't worry about any small pieces of charcoal left in the water. A small amount will do your stomach more good than harm.

Medical

If you are planning to walk through mountainous or remote countryside, thorough preparation is essential. Even on a fine summer day, the weather can change rapidly and mist or fog can reduce visibility to just a few metres. It is easy to underestimate how difficult a walk in a mountainous area might be, or how dangerous rocky ground can be. If you do get into difficulties or injure yourself, it may be some time before you can raise the alarm and the emergency services can reach you.

Although many hillwalkers prefer to keep their own company, one should never venture alone into a remote area. You may be adequately dressed, have the proper footwear, and a rucksack full of camping equipment, but this will mean little if you fall and injure yourself. Lying unconscious in the cold and wet leaves little time for a search party to discover you missing and then find you – hypothermia kills very quickly. Likewise, some injuries, such as uncontrolled bleeding, can also be life-threatening. If you do decide to walk alone, always leave a copy of your route and an estimated time you can be expected back. Some mountainous areas have radio relays positioned on them so it is worth considering taking your mobile phone along. If it does work, and you have an accident, it could save your life.

Some of the procedures described in this section are complex and it may be possible to obtain more information and practical advice from a local branch of the Ambulance Association or Red Cross (see page 192). Some organizations run first-aid sessions.

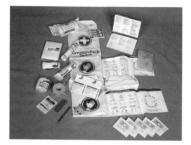

FIRST-AID KIT

There are many first-aid packs on the market, most of which contain a few plasters and the odd bandage. However, there is one first-aid pack which has been specifically designed for the outdoor enthusiast – the Gregson Lifesaver System. The Gregson pack has been designed to help perform first-aid procedures as you read aloud the instructions, which saves vital seconds. The instructions are easy to follow and the contents easy to find, covering all eventualities from blisters to bleeding, fractures to burns, and even rescue.

If you prefer to assemble your own personal medical first-aid kit, consider what items you will include. The range of survival equipment is vast, with new items coming onto the market every year. However, there are several vital questions you should ask yourself about each item. Is it really necessary? Is its function duplicated by any other item? Are you capable of using the item? Remember – the aim is to keep the kit as small as possible. Once selected, assemble all the pieces of equipment you intend to carry and make sure they are well packed in a totally waterproof container. The simplest way of ensuring the latter is to seal the whole kit in an airtight, plastic, snap-seal food container. Once packed and closed, the container should be sealed with adhesive polythene tape.

The items chosen for the kit should reflect your first-aid skill and should include the following basic items:

- **Plasters.** A good selection of assorted plasters, but err on the large size, as they can be cut down as required. Use the waterproof type.

- **Suture plasters.** A strip of butterfly sutures is ideal for closing small wounds.

- **Needles and safety pins.** Various sizes.

- **Medical wipes.** Two strips.

- **Paraffin burn dressing.**

- **Large wound dressings.** Always carry at least one large wound dressing.

- **Aspirin.** At least two dozen soluble aspirins will serve to relieve mild pain and headaches. They can also reduce fever.

- **Diarrhoea powder and rehydration mix.**

- **Antihistamine cream.** Insect bites and stings can cause severe irritation.
- **All-purpose antiseptic cream.**
- **Water purification tablets.** You will need two dozen.
- **Small pair of scissors.**
- **Salt.** A small container of salt should be carried if the climate is very hot.
- **A small first-aid book.** *Gem First Aid* is ideal, in terms of both content and portability.

BREATHING MEANS LIFE

It is often said that we can live without food for weeks, water for four days and air for four minutes. I am not so sure about the duration for food and water, but the figure for air is certainly correct. The brain needs oxygen which means the first thing you must look for is a sign of life. This means that in an emergency you should immediately check that the casualty is breathing and that a pulse is detectable. The first point indicates that the airway is clear and the second that blood is flowing around the body – at this stage nothing else is important.

AUTHOR'S NOTE

It's a little old-fashioned now, but I always remember the ABC – Airway, Breathing, Circulation.

CHOKING AND A CLEAR AIRWAY

The first priority for anyone who is not breathing or who is in immediate danger of not breathing (through choking) is to get them breathing either freely or by artificial respiration. Casualties showing serious signs of choking need immediate assistance to clear the airway. These signs may include being unable to speak or breathe, the skin going pale blue, or the casualty grasping his throat. The condition is usually caused by something lodged in the windpipe, which prevents the free passage of air to the lungs.

Removal of the obstruction is an urgent requirement. A conscious survivor should be encouraged to cough it away. If this is ineffective, check inside the mouth to see if the blockage can be cleared with your finger. If the choking continues, gravity and slapping should be tried to shake it free. Do this by helping the casualty to bend forward so that the head is below lung level. Now slap the casualty sharply between the shoulder blades, using the heel of your hand. This may be repeated three more times if necessary. Check inside the mouth and remove the obstruction if it has been freed. If it has not, try to clear it using air pressure generated by abdominal thrusts.

ABDOMINAL THRUSTS

In order to administer abdominal thrusts, you should follow the correct procedure. If the casualty is conscious and upright, stand behind him and put your arms around his waist. Clench one fist and place it with the thumb side against his abdomen. Make sure it is resting between his naval and the lower end of the breastbone. Place your other hand over the fist. Make a firm thrust upwards and into the abdomen. Do this up to four times if required. Pause after each thrust and be prepared to remove anything dislodged from the air passage. Should the choking still persist, repeat the four back slaps and the four abdominal thrusts alternately until the obstruction is cleared.

An unconscious casualty requiring abdominal thrusts must be turned on his back. Kneeling astride him, place the heel of one hand between the navel and breastbone, and put the other hand on top. Deliver the four thrusts as above. If the obstruction persists, and the patient stops breathing, begin assisted breathing and chest compression as above.

If you have very small children with you on your walk, make sure you know how to treat them accordingly. The techniques mentioned above are designed for adults and could cause serious damage to a small child.

CHECK BREATHING

To determine if an unconscious casualty is breathing, listen with your ear close to the nose and mouth. You should be able to hear and feel any breath. Watch out for chest and abdominal movement at the same time. If there is no sign of breathing, take immediate action to ensure that the air passages are clear.

If the injured person is unconscious, it may be that the airway is blocked by the position of the head (**a**). To remedy this, press down on the forehead with one hand, and with the other lift the neck (**b**). Remove your hand from underneath the neck to push up the chin (**c**), to stop the tongue blocking the top of the airway. If there is still

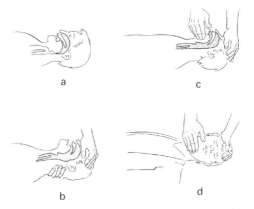

a

c

b

d

no breathing, there may be an obstruction in the airway. Turn the head to one side, keeping the chin forward and the top of the head back (**d**). Check quickly inside the mouth to find and remove any other cause of blockage, e.g. dentures, vomit. Once the air passage is open and clear, the casualty may begin breathing again. If this happens, and his heart is beating, put him into the coma (or recovery) position (illustrated on page 133). If there is a visible injury to the front or back of the head (which might indicate damage to the neck or spine), maintain the clear airway with the head back. Improvise some form of collar or head support to keep the head correctly positioned.

ARTIFICIAL RESPIRATION

If breathing does not recommence, the casualty must be given help with respiration. This can best be done on a mouth-to-mouth basis. Taking a deep breath, pinch the casualty's nose to prevent air loss, open your mouth wide and seal your lips around his open mouth. Blow into his lungs, watching for expansion of the chest. When the maximum expansion is reached, raise your head well clear and breathe out and in. Look now for the chest contraction. When this has happened, repeat the procedure four times.

Following the fourth assisted breath, it is important to check that the casualty's heart is beating. The oxygen, having been taken up by the blood, must be delivered to the body's vital organs. Feel for the carotid pulse, in the neck.

If there is no heartbeat, chest compression must be carried out as described below. **Be sure that there is no heartbeat before beginning chest compression.** Far more harm than good will be done if attempted chest compression interferes with an existing heartbeat, however weak.

If the heart is beating, continue giving assisted breaths at between sixteen and eighteen a minute. When the casualty begins breathing for himself, continue giving assistance at his natural rate until breathing is normal. Then place him in the coma (recovery) position.

CHEST COMPRESSIONS

Check that the casualty is lying on a firm surface. Kneeling alongside, locate the bottom of the breastbone (**a**). Measure the width of three fingers up and place the heel of one hand on the bone. Lay the other hand over the first (**b**). Keeping the elbows rigid, lean forward so that your arms are vertical and your weight is bearing down on the casualty's chest (**c**). Depress the breastbone by between 4 and 5 cm (2 in). Lean back to release the pressure, allowing the breastbone to return to its original

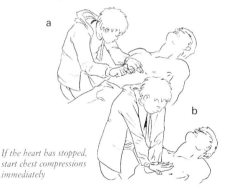

If the heart has stopped, start chest compressions immediately

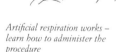

position. Perform fifteen compressions at the rate of about eighty per minute. (Count, **One back, two back, three back,** and so on, leaning forward on each number.)

In normal conditions, breathing and blood circulation take place at the same time. The casualty needs both, so artificial respiration (see page 130) and chest compression must be carried out together

Artificial respiration works – learn how to administer the procedure

(**d**). If you are alone, the procedures have to be alternated. As soon as the first fifteen compressions have been given, restore the open air passage position of the head and provide two more assisted breaths. When this has been done, continue this cycle: fifteen compressions and two assisted breaths for a full minute. Check for any heartbeat. If none is present, continue the treatment, checking for a heartbeat every three minutes.

If two active survivors are available they should each provide part of the treatment, one assisting breathing and the other providing the compressions. At the start, give four assisted breaths and follow these with five compressions. Then establish a pattern of one assisted breath followed by five compressions. Aim at a rate of one compression per second. Each assisted breath should follow the release of the fifth compression without a pause. The check for the heartbeat should be made after one minute and then after every succeeding three minutes. Stop the compressions when a pulse is felt. Continue with assisted breathing until the casualty breathes for himself. When breathing and heartbeat are both established, check for other injuries and place the casualty in the coma position (see below).

THE COMA OR RECOVERY POSITION

Generally, an unconscious survivor who is breathing, who has a reasonable heartbeat and who is without other injuries demanding immediate attention, should be put

Place an unconscious person, who is breathing normally and has a regular heart beat, in the coma position

into the coma (or recovery) position. This position, illustrated below, is the safest because it minimizes the risk of impeded breathing. The tilted-back head ensures open air passages. The face-down attitude allows any vomit or other liquid obstruction to drain from the mouth.

The spread of the limbs will maintain the body in its position. If fractures or other injuries prevent suitable placing of the limbs, use rolled clothing or other padded objects to prop the survivor in this position.

MEDICAL EMERGENCIES

The ability to carry out first aid has enormous value in normal circumstances. This knowledge is beyond measure in an emergency, and where there may be no quick prospect of skilled assistance. Your medical supplies may be inadequate or entirely absent, but if you can provide first aid for yourself or others, even if only limited, it can help save lives.

As in every other aspect of an emergency, there is a need for assessment and for priorities to be established. Once it has been established that the casualty is breathing freely, examine what is medically wrong. Normally the situation itself will give a pretty good idea of what injuries to look for, but whatever the circumstances, keep these general rules in mind:

- Keep calm. However serious an injury or dangerous a situation, panic will impair the ability to think and so lower your effectiveness. Time will be wasted – and time can mean life.

- Avoid any unnecessary danger to yourself. This is not cowardice. You will be no help to anybody if you also suffer needless injury.

- Think carefully before you act.

- Do your best to reassure and comfort any casualty. Try to provide the sort of encouragement from which the will to live will grow.

- Find out if there are any other uninjured or active survivors who can help to deal with the situation. In particular, look for anyone with medical qualifications or better experience than your own.

- When assessing individual casualties, use your own senses to the full. **Ask. Look. Listen. Smell.** Then **Think** and **Act**.

- If the casualty is conscious, ask them to describe their symptoms, and to tell you what they think happened and what they feel is wrong. If there are others present, check if anyone has anything relevant to add.

BLEEDING

The body contains about nine pints of blood. Damage to the body can cause blood loss, which if unchecked will weaken the circulation and blood supply to the brain. Blood will clot relatively quickly if the flow is slowed or stopped, and although a cleanly-cut blood vessel may bleed profusely if left untreated, it will also tend to shrink, close and retreat into its surrounding tissue. Sometimes these natural methods will succeed in arresting bleeding entirely unaided.

It is not uncommon for hillwalkers or campers to suffer minor wounds and abrasions; these should be cleaned and dressed. Any other major wound which causes severe bleeding should be stopped as soon as possible. There are three options available.

DIRECT PRESSURE

Place a dressing over the wound and apply firm but gentle pressure with your hand. A sterile dressing is desirable (**a**). If one is not available, any piece of clean cloth can be used. If no dressing is ready for immediate use, cover the wound with your hand. If necessary, hold the edges of the wound together using only gentle pressure. Any dressings should be large enough to overlap the wound and cover the surrounding area (**b**). If

Stop any bleeding by applying direct pressure to the wound. Apply several bandages if necessary

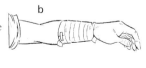

blood comes through the first dressing, apply a second over the first, and, if required, a third over the second. Keep an even pressure applied by tying on a firm bandage. However, take care that the bandage is not so tight that, like a tourniquet, it restricts the flow of blood.

If the wound is large and suitable dressings are to hand, bring the edges of the wound together and use the dressings to keep the wound closed (**c**). To arrest the flow of blood from a very large wound, make a pad of the dressing and press it into the wound where the bleeding is heaviest. The object of this

treatment is to slow down or stop the loss of blood until the body's own defences begin to work.

ELEVATION

If there is no danger of any other injury being aggravated, an injured limb is best raised as high as is comfortable for the casualty (**d**). This reduces the blood-flow in the limb, helps the veins to drain the area and so assists in reducing the blood-loss through the wound.

Elevating the limb will help reduce the blood flow

INDIRECT PRESSURE

If a combination of the above procedures does not succeed, the use of appropriate pressure points should be considered. It is necessary to recognize the type of external bleeding, because pressure points can only be used to control arterial bleeding. Arteries carry the blood outwards from the heart, in pulses of pressure. At this stage, the blood has been oxygenated and filtered of its impurities. Arterial bleeding can therefore be recognized by bright-red spurting in time with each heartbeat. In contrast, blood from the veins flows out steadily, with less pressure, and is a darker red.

A place where an artery runs across a bone near the surface of the skin constitutes a pressure point. There are four pressure points which are easily accessible to control heavy arterial bleeding, one in each limb. Those in the arms are on the brachial arteries. These run down the centre of the inner side of the upper arm (**a**). Pressure points for the legs are on the femoral arteries, which run down the inside of each thigh (**b**). The pressure points can be found in the centre of the groin, and can be

Indirect pressure can help stop severe arterial bleeding – a knowledge of the body's pressure points is essential

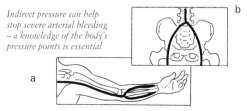

b

a

compressed against the pelvis. This is easier to do if the casualty's knee is bent. When using pressure points to control bleeding, make full use of the opportunity to dress the wound more effectively.

PRESSURE APPLICATION

Locate the fingers or thumb over the pressure point and apply sufficient pressure to flatten the artery and arrest the flow of blood. Redress the wound if required.

Maintain the pressure for at least ten minutes to allow time for blood-clotting to begin. **Do not exceed fifteen minutes.** If you do, the tissues below the pressure point will begin to be damaged by the deprivation of arterial blood.

INTERNAL BLEEDING

Internal bleeding is often difficult to spot, but should be suspected if the casualty has had a hard fall on rocky ground, breaking ribs or thigh bones without external rupture of the skin. Blood appearing in the mouth, ears and nose from no obvious wound is a likely indicator, as is any excessive swelling or bruising. There is little first aid that can be applied to a casualty with internal bleeding. The best course of action is to get them to hospital as soon as possible. If you do suspect internal bleeding, treat the casualty for shock until help arrives.

SHOCK

In the context of first aid, 'shock' relates to surgical shock and has nothing to do with being frightened. Surgical shock is caused by a loss of blood circulating through the body. This causes the pressure to fall, thus inhibiting the supply of oxygen to the brain, and organs such as the heart and kidneys. The system is clever enough to monitor any blood-loss from the body and will shut down all nonessential arteries, enabling the heart and brain to operate – but there is a limit. Casualties suspected of going into shock need to be hospitalized as quickly as possible.

If you suspect shock, make sure that you carry out the following:

- Lie the casualty down and drop the head a little, allowing blood to the brain.
- Do not let the casualty move, and decrease all pressure on the heart.
- Cover the casualty very lightly. Getting the casualty too warm will only divert blood to the body's outer surface.
- Stop any bleeding.
- If the casualty is vomiting, place him in the coma or recovery position (see page 133).
- If breathing stops, begin artificial respiration (see page 130). Raise the legs to increase blood supply to the heart and brain.

FRACTURES

A fracture is a broken or cracked bone, which, depending on the type, may be accompanied by internal or external bleeding.

A closed fracture is not immediately obvious, although there will be swelling and bruising (**a**). An open fracture is where the broken bone has ruptured the skin, thus exposing the wound to infection (**b**). A complicated fracture may be open or closed, but where the broken bone has caused injury to nerves, arteries and other organs (**c**).

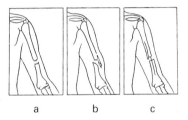

a   b   c

A bone fracture should be suspected if someone has had a serious fall and if any or all of the following signs are present:

- The bone is exposed through the skin.
- There is difficulty of normal movement in any part of the body.
- Increased pain when movement is attempted.
- Swelling or bruising accompanied by tenderness in the area of the injury.
- Deformity or shortening of the injured part.

- Grating of bone heard during examination or attempted movement.
- Signs of shock.
- The casualty has heard or felt a bone break.

The only treatment available in an emergency situation is immobilization of the fracture. Unless some other immediate danger threatens, splint the casualty before moving him. In any case, handle him with the greatest care to avoid further pain or additional injury. If there is a wound associated with the fracture, remove the clothing in the immediate area and treat the wound before fitting splints.

Splints can be improvised from sticks and branches, or even a tight roll of clothing or bedding. Pad the splint and fasten it so that it supports the joints above and below the fracture. A fractured leg can be partially immobilized by tying it to the good leg if nothing else is available. A fractured leg may be deformed, shortened or twisted unnaturally. In such cases realignment should be attempted before immobilization, if the casualty is prepared to allow it. Carefully and gently pull the end of the limb and reset or straighten it. When all that is possible has been done, apply the splints.

The only further help that can be given is to raise the injured part to cut down swelling and discomfort, and to treat any symptoms of shock. If it is not possible to move the casualty, he should be allowed to rest. If it is considered that the casualty is capable of being moved, and that this provides the best way of the casualty receiving prompt hospitalization, then this should be done.

CARRYING AN INJURED PERSON

A moderately injured person should be carried between two helpers, using whichever handgrip suits best or by a fireman's lift. The lifts illustrated below are the four-handed seat (**a**), used when the injured person can use his arms, and the two-handed seat (**b**), for when the injured person is unable to use his arms. Another option is to empty a rucksack and extend the shoulder straps to the limit. It is then possible to piggy-back the casualty by threading his legs through the straps of the rucksack by getting him to hold onto you around your neck. This is only viable, though, if the casualty is able to hold on. However, a more seriously injured person, if they must be moved, should be moved in such a way as not to

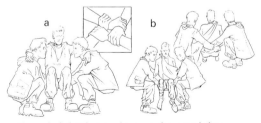

Always check that the injured person is fit to carry before attempting any lift

endanger their health or worsen their injuries further. In these cases, a stretcher, even an improvised one, should be used. A makeshift stretcher can be improvised by threading two jackets on a pole or branch, with a belt to give more stability at the middle (**a**). If you have to lift a patient to get them on a stretcher, make sure that the body is in line and that each part is well supported, i.e. that the centre isn't sagging (**b**). If a patient has any suspected spinal injuries, do not attempt to move them.

a

b

CONCUSSION AND SKULL FRACTURES

If a survivor is even briefly unconscious, if clear or blood-tinged fluid is coming from the ears or nose, or if the pupils of the eyes are unequal or unresponsive, then a skull fracture or concussion should be suspected. If the casualty is unconscious, breathing and pulse should be monitored. If they are normal, the casualty should be placed in the coma position. If the casualty is conscious, place him in a reclining position with his head and shoulders supported, keep him warm and handle him gently.

BURNS

The immediate aim when treating any burn is to lessen the ill effects of the excessive heat. Do this by gently immersing the injured part in cold water or by slowly pouring cold water over it. Persist with this treatment for ten minutes, or longer if the pain is not relieved. Cooling in this way will stop further damage, relieve pain and reduce the possibilities of swelling or shock.

A burn opens the way for infection to enter the body, which means that a dressing should be applied. A sterile non-fluffy dressing is best, but any suitable piece of clean material will do. Dressings and bandages can be made fairly sterile by boiling, or by steaming them in a lidded container. Scorching of material will also help to kill most germs.

A solution of tannic acid will assist in the healing of burns. Tree bark boiled for as long as possible will provide this. Oak bark is the best source, but chestnut is a good alternative. Any bark will yield some tannic acid. As the water boils away, replace it with more, adding extra bark if possible. A strong-tea solution will provide the same assistance. Cool the boiled tannic acid by placing the container in cold water. Do not use any solution until it is cold.

If any restrictive clothing or other items are being worn near the burned area, remove them before any swelling develops. Do not touch the burn or use any form of adhesive dressing. If any blisters form, do not break or drain them. They are a natural protective cover for the injury and should themselves be protected. If burns or scalds are severe, lay the casualty in a comfortable position as soon as possible. If the casualty is unconscious, place him in the coma or recovery position (see page 133). Be aware that the patient may also go into shock (see page 139).

SUNBURN

The most likely type of burn to be encountered will be sunburn. Over-exposure to direct sunlight, especially when combined with persistent wind, can produce serious burning. Skin, wet with seawater or sweat, is similarly at risk. If sunburn does occur, protect the casualty from further exposure. Treat the area with tannic acid solution (or ointment if available), or with cold water if in plentiful supply. Then cover with a dressing. Keep the dressing in place unless it is essential that it be removed. Provide the survivor with plenty of fluids (as much as possible) and rest.

HEAT EXHAUSTION

The constant need for water arises from the fact that the body is continually releasing liquids during its normal functions, i.e. breathing, urination, excretion and sweating. It is possible for hillwalkers to suffer from heat exhaustion, which is normally caused by excessive sweating due to hot weather and arduous routes. The simple cure for this complaint is to rest in the shade, cooling the head with a water-drenched cloth while replenishing body fluids with small mouthfuls of water.

Of secondary importance to water is salt. The normal human requires 10 g each day to maintain a healthy balance. Sweat contains salt as well as water, and this salt-loss must be replaced. If it is not then you will suffer from heatstroke, heat exhaustion and muscular cramps.

The signs of salt deficiency are sudden weakness and a hot dry sensation to the body. Placing the victim in a half-lying, half-sitting position (**a**), and adding a small pinch of salt to a mug of water, will eliminate these feelings very quickly (**b**). Fanning will also cool down the victim effectively (**c**). In hot, dry hillwalking

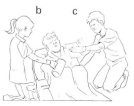

conditions it is advisable to add a small amount of salt to your entire fluid intake.

In any situation where good water might be in short supply, the first step is to protect and conserve the water already in the body. This is done by covering any exposed skin as soon as possible. This will not only give protection against sunburn, but it will also aid water retention. Rest and avoid energetic activities until you have fully recovered. Don't smoke, or drink alcohol.

All these actions, however effective they may be, are only short-term responses to the main problem. Long-term survival depends on a good supply of drinkable water (see section on Water, page 118). Without it, survival prospects are nonexistent unless rescue intervenes. Without water, anything else – food, equipment, shelter, fire, etc. – is worth very little.

KEEPING WARM

Exposure to temperatures below freezing, especially if it is wet and windy, entails continual risk of hypothermia and frostbite. Windy conditions increase the risk of hypothermia because the cooling effects of cold air are markedly increased by its movement. Air moving at 48 km/h (30 mph) and having a temperature of –20 °C (–4 °F) has the same chilling effect as air at –40 °C (–40 °F) moving at only 8 km/h (5 mph). Wet conditions increase the danger because wet cold air is a better conductor of heat, and can therefore carry more away from the body. In addition, many of the insulating properties of clothing are lost if garments are wet or damp.

Make the most efficient use of all available clothing. Remember that a number of thinner layers are more effective than one or two thick heavy garments in preventing loss of body heat. The aim is to maintain a layer of unchanging air close to your body. Tight clothing should therefore be avoided. Adjust your clothing so as to reduce sweating. Too much perspiration lowers the insulating efficiency of clothing, as well as cooling the skin as the sweat evaporates. Remove layers of clothing and/or open garments at the front, wrist or neck to get the right balance. Do everything possible to prevent clothing getting wet, and do all you can to dry it if it does get wet.

Take special care of hands and feet. They are the limits of circulation and can lose heat very rapidly. Do everything possible to ensure that the fastenings at wrists, ankles, neck and around the waist are efficient without restricting the circulation of blood. Keep hands under cover whenever possible, warming them under the armpits or between the thighs when necessary. If toes are nipped by frost, warm them against a companion if possible. If alone, warm toes by wriggling them, moving the feet and, providing there are no serious signs, gentle massage.

Make every effort to keep feet dry. If spare socks are available, keep some close to hand so that a change into a dry pair can be made at least once a day. Periodically remove footwear and rub your feet for up to ten minutes. Try to improvise over-boots using plastic bags placed over walking boots to ensure extra insulation against cold and wet.

HYPOTHERMIA

This general condition of the body is caused when it loses heat more quickly than heat can be replaced. Among the conditions likely to produce an increased risk of hypothermia are cold, wet weather, wet clothing, immersion in cold water, exhaustion, inadequate clothing and a shortage of food or drink. Hypothermia is not an easily-diagnosed condition. It is important, therefore, to keep a special lookout if you are subject to any of these conditions. Signs of hypothermia include:

- Paleness and severe uncontrollable shivering.
- Being subnormally cold to the touch.
- Muscular weakness and fatigue.
- Drowsiness and dimming of sight.
- Diminishing heartbeat and breathing.
- Eventual collapse and unconsciousness (extremely serious).

In addition to the signs listed above, perhaps the most striking indication of the onset of hypothermia is that of a marked change in the personality of the sufferer. An extrovert may become an introvert. Aggressiveness may change to submission, or vice versa. What is certain is that hypothermia is deadly unless it is treated. The treatment of hypothermia is centred on stopping the loss of body heat and replacing lost warmth.

There are two other actions to remember if hypothermia is encountered. If both breathing and heartbeat are undetectable, artificial respiration (see page 130) and chest compressions (see page 131) will need to be administered. Do not assume death from hypothermia, unless your efforts have achieved normal body temperature and the casualty still does not revive. Handle any hypothermia survivor gently. Frozen skin and flesh are very easily damaged. When hypothermia is detected:

- **Do not** rub or massage to stimulate circulation.
- **Do not** warm the casualty by using external fire or heat.
- **Do not** permit the casualty further exertion.
- Provide shelter from the wind and cold as soon as possible.
- If dry clothing or covering is available, use it to replace any wet clothing.
- Replace wet clothing in stages, uncovering as little of the body as possible at any one time.
- If no dry clothing is available, leave any wet garments on and get the casualty into a sleeping bag or survival bag (**a**, see page 152). It should be wind- and waterproof, as well as being reflective of radiated body heat.

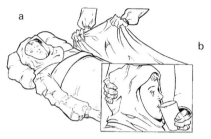

Hypothermia is a real killer – learn to spot the signs and prevent further deterioration

- Provide body warmth. Another healthy survivor is a good source and can share the survival bag. If the casualty is conscious, provide hot food and drink (**b**). If none is available, eat chocolate or high-energy food. **Do not** give alcohol.

AUTHOR'S NOTE

I cannot stress enough the importance of protecting yourself against hypothermia. It has taken the lives of many hillwalkers, due mainly to the rapidity with which the body's temperature falls during wet, windy and cold conditions. Even experienced SAS soldiers have fallen victim to hypothermia.

CRAMP

The onset of cramp is very sudden and starts with an involuntary contraction of the lower leg muscles, normally those in the calf. They can occur at any time, but are most prevalent after very strenuous exercise, when you are resting. Cramps are more frequent after walking in hot weather, when heavy sweating has occurred. Although extremely painful, the condition is not serious and the pain will dissipate within a few minutes. First of all, any joint that is bent by the cramping muscles should be gently straightened (**a**). Massaging the affected area with a gentle stroking movement should then help to relieve the tension (**b**).

Cramps are best treated by gentle massaging

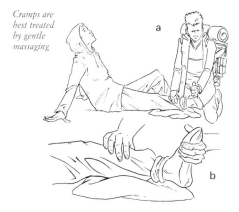

BLISTERS

Normally, blisters are considered a minor injury and are treated as such. However, when out walking the pain of a blister can become disabling and out of all proportion to its medical significance. Blisters on the feet are usually caused by ill-fitting boots, poor-quality socks or loose laces combined with long periods of having to walk over rough, uneven ground.

Bad blisters can be avoided. First of all, the feet must be kept clean and dry, washed whenever possible, dried thoroughly and foot powder applied. If you notice sore spots on your feet while walking, put some surgical spirit on them to toughen them up.

As soon as you feel a blister beginning, stop immediately and treat the problem. Put some antiseptic cream on the sore area and then cover it with surgical dressing, without making any creases in the tape. If the sore area is on a toe, use micropore tape instead. If a blister has already formed, use a blister ring so that pressure is kept off the affected area.

A severe blister is often filled with fluid, and can be made more comfortable if the fluid is removed. To do this, do not burst it, as this leaves a larger area open to infection, but pierce it at the bottom edge using a sterilized needle. If possible, wash the foot thoroughly first, then gently express the fluid and cover the blister with a blister ring. Make sure that the dressing is changed daily and the area cleaned. A footbath of hot, salty water is healing, comforting and helps to harden the skin. However, make sure that the area is thoroughly dried. Blisters heal best when they are kept clean and dry.

HYGIENE AND SANITATION

With modern sanitation, we often take a lot for granted. However, out in the wilds completely different rules apply, both to protect the environment and your health. Any toilet waste should be disposed of in a hole at least 15 cm (6 in) deep and as far away as possible from any water sources. Afterwards, replace the soil and any turf and tread down well. All personal and clothes washing, too, should be done well away from a water source.

Bodily cleanliness is a major protection against disease, germs and infestations. A daily wash with warm water and soap is the ideal. If this is not possible, concentrate on keeping the hands clean, and wash and sponge the face, armpits, crotch and feet at least once a day.

Clothing, especially underclothing, must be kept as clean and dry as possible. At the very least, shake out clothing and expose it to the sun and air each day.

Your teeth should be examined on a regular basis. This will avoid any unpleasant toothache while you are out walking. Protect your teeth by brushing them at least twice a day. An improvised toothpick can be made from the crushed end of a small twig. It is possible to use charcoal ash as tooth powder.

PRECAUTIONS AGAINST THINGS THAT BITE

No hillwalker should make the mistake of thinking that the greatest danger comes from large animals. Britain has little wild game, few snakes or other reptiles. If anything, it is the smaller forms of wildlife that should give most cause for concern. Any insect bite is potentially dangerous.

Mosquitoes

Mosquitoes, while not particularly dangerous in the Arctic and temperate regions, can be deadly in the

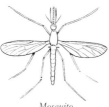

Mosquito

Tropics. They can carry malaria, yellow fever and filariasis. Do everything possible to gain protection against their bites. Use mosquito netting or repellent constantly if it is available. If not, cover any exposed skin with handkerchiefs or anything else to hand. Even large leaves will help. Wear full clothing, especially at night. Keep trouser legs tucked into the tops of socks and shirt sleeves into gloves or other improvised hand covering. Smear the face and other exposed skin with mud before bedding down for the night.

Select rest sites or camps which are clear of and higher than swampy ground or stagnant or sluggish water, since this is where mosquitoes breed. Establish a slow smoky fire to windward of the camp site. Keep it burning to drive insects away. Put a ring of ash around all bed spaces to deter most crawling insects.

There is no immunization against malaria, so any anti-malaria drugs must be used as directed for as long as they last.

BITING GNATS AND MIDGES

Apart from the irritation caused by clouds of midges hovering around your head, there are several species of blook-sucking gnats that feed on livestock. These are of particular importance as they can transmit disease from animals to humans, though this is rare in the Western world.

AVOIDING MIDGES

Stay away from areas which have recently housed livestock, especially during the hours of dusk. Likewise, avoiding any standing water as this is a common breeding ground for gnats and midges. A liberal layer of insect repellent will normally stop any actual bites, but in areas of high infestation you might consider covering any exposed skin, such as the face, with a fine mesh hood.

TICKS

Ticks are crawling creatures measuring between 2 mm and 1 cm. They are blooksuckers and possess strong piercing jaws, and are responsible for most of the world's transmittable diseases. There are two families of ticks which are able to transmit disease to humans.

Soft ticks hide in dilapidated buildings with poor hygiene. They usually are active at night and bite sleeping people, in order to suck blood. Soft ticks can live for many years. When they find a host they usually stay attached for less than 30 minutes.

Hard ticks normally feed on animals, e.g. dogs, goats, rats, sheep, cattle, onto which they climb from the ground or vegetation. Hard ticks have a two-year life cycle, starting with the egg and continuing through the six-legged larva or seed tick, the eight-legged immature nymph to the eight-legged mature adult. They remain attached to the animal and suck blood for many days, and in doing so they carry tick typhus from animals to humans.

AVOIDING TICKS

Preventing ticks from attaching themselves to you is the best way of avoiding tick-implanted disease. Unless it is an emergency, you should not sleep in old buildings which have housed livestock. If you are camping out, ensure that the vegetation around the tent is kept short. Hard ticks are the most common but any disease will not be transferred if the tick is removed within 24 hours. Most DEET insect repellents are very effective against ticks.

REMOVING A TICK

The best method of removal is to grasp the skin area around the tick's body with a pair of fine-point tweezers, and remove the tick with a sharp backwards pull.

Despite this sounding quite painful, it will not hurt and is a far safer method than trying to induce the tick to disengage itself by any other method. Burning the tick or applying chemicals will only force the tick to vomit, and crushing it will cause germs to enter the victim.

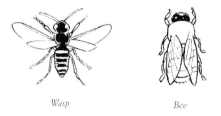

Wasp

Bee

FLIES, BEES, WASPS AND HORNETS

There are many species of fly, and they vary widely in the sorts of diseases they transmit. However, good camp and personal hygiene will prevent most contamination. All bees, wasps and hornets are very dangerous if aroused. Nests are generally brownish oval or oblong masses, on tree trunks or branches between 3 m (9 ft) and 10 m (30 ft) above ground. Avoid them if possible. If a swarm is disturbed, and you are nearby, sit still for five minutes or so, and then crawl away slowly and carefully. Should you be attacked, run through the bushiest undergrowth you can find. This will beat off the insects as it springs back. Immersion in water is another defence.

SNAKES

In the UK there is only one species of poisonous snake – the adder. In America the coral snake, copperhead, rattlesnake and cottonmouth are the snakes which should concern the walker. A snake-bite is seldom life-threatening, but you should take a number of precautions just to be on the safe side. As snakes strike at ankle level you should wear boots and socks which protect the lower part of your leg. In America in particular, ensure that you do not walk at night, as snakes are nocturnal. They also like to seek out warm places at night, so a tent is far preferable to sleeping out under the stars. In the unlikely event of being bitten by a snake, the best thing to do is to tie a bandage above the bite, then gradually cover the bite with the bandage and tie it again firmly below the bite. Get medical assistance as soon as possible, and certainly within twelve hours.

BEARS

America is home to black bears and grizzly bears. In both cases it is best to avoid them if at all possible. You can do this by making a noise such as singing or talking as you are walking along, and by avoiding anything which looks like rotting food, as this may well be a bear larder.

If you encounter a bear, do not look it in the eye. If it turns sideways on to you or starts to shake its head from side to side, it is inviting you to leave. Move away very slowly and very quietly. Never run, as a grizzly bear can run far faster than you. Often, a bear charge will in fact be a bluff. Standing absolutely still may well help your cause. As a last resort, play dead by rolling yourself into a ball, drawing your legs up into your torso and covering your neck with your hands.

When looking for an appropriate camping site, keep bears in mind. It is best if the tent, cooking site and food storage site are all at some distance from each other. Food can be stored in large metal lockers at popular camp sites, or portable bear-resistant food containers can be purchased and carried with you. There is also the option of fashioning your own bear-bag storage system by suspending your rucksack from a branch of a tree, preferably about 7 m (21 ft) above the ground, and keeping it there by counterbalancing it with a rock attached to the opposite end of a piece of rope.

POISONOUS PLANTS

In America poison ivy, poison oak and poison sumac all cause skin irritation. If your skin comes into contact with any of these plants, you should wash the affected area with soap and water, and remove and wash any affected clothing. Remember not to touch any other parts of your skin or face until you have thoroughly washed. If you are very allergic, and the rash persists for a number of weeks, see a doctor who will prescribe drugs which should help combat the symptoms.

The Weather

The weather in the British Isles is unpredictable at best and this is doubly so on hilltops and mountains. Weather can cause many problems and potential dangers for hillwalkers, so you must be aware of sudden changes at all times and be prepared to act accordingly. Although we cannot change the weather, we can to a certain extent predict it.

Before undertaking any hillwalking trip, the weather forecast for the region should be checked. Any weather conditions that are liable to cause exposure and frostbite or heat-stroke are good reasons for postponing your activity. Always use common sense and try to interpret prevailing weather conditions in the light of the most up-to-date forecast. This becomes even more important in winter. Fatalities which occur as a result of the weather often involve some human carelessness or ignorance; both can be avoided. If the worst happens and you do find yourself and your party trapped on a hill or mountain in bad weather, find shelter, keep together and sit it out. As long as clothing and food are adequate and morale is high, you will stand a good chance of survival. You should be aware that the weather can pose a whole range of problems for the hillwalker.

Heavy rain can cause streams to become fast and swollen. Trying to negotiate a swollen stream is risky to say the least, and potentially life-threatening. Find another route if necessary to detour around it (see page 76).

Fog can be dangerous as it is disorientating and hides obstacles and hazards, such as cliff-edges. In such terrain and conditions you are best advised to stay put until the visibility improves. If you have to keep going, consider roping the members of the party together. In this way you can be assured that no one will get lost and it may also save someone from a nasty fall.

Wind gusts, especially in exposed places such as a high ridge-line, can be so powerful as to knock a person off their feet. If there is any danger of this, get all party members to crawl on their hands and knees and keep them close together. Again, it may be necessary to rope everyone together.

Hailstones can be up to 2 cm (1 in) in diameter and rain down with sufficient force to cause serious injury. In the rare event of being caught out in a hailstorm, make sure you find shelter or at least cover your head.

It is wise to take precautions against lightning while hillwalking. However, it is very rare for an electrical storm to occur without some advance warning. The appearance of thunderclouds in the distance followed by flashes of lightning and rumbles of thunder are all good indicators. Watch the direction in which the clouds are moving. Note that lightning strikes the easiest point with which to make contact, which is usually the highest point in the area. If you are caught out in a lightning storm, it is much safer to stay out in the open, even if it is in driving rain. Sit down, preferably on your rucksack, and minimize your contact points with the ground by drawing your knees up and placing your hands in your lap.

WEATHER FORECASTS

In addition to the national television, radio and newspaper weather forecasts, hillwalkers have access to a number of other forecasting services.

Weathercall offers forecasts by telephone or by fax. For instance, to get a regional telephone forecast for northwest Scotland, you should ring 0891 500 425, for north Wales 0891 500 415 and for the Lake District 0891 500 419. Similarly, fax forecasts are available for these areas by typing 0897 300 1, plus the appropriate suffix (northwest Scotland is 25), into the fax machine. Weathercall also provides a national seven-day forecast by phone on 0891 500 400. Regional long-range forecasts are also available.

There are also specialized weather forecasts for hillwalkers. BBC Radio Scotland has a daily forecast at 6.55 pm (weekdays) and 6.05 pm (weekends), and in winter this includes an avalanche risk assessment as well. ClimbLine provides regional forecasts for the Western Highlands of Scotland on 0891 333 198 and the Eastern Highlands on 0891 333 197. Most youth hostels in mountainous areas get a faxed daily forecast from the Met Office.

AUTHOR'S NOTE

I have found a method of anticipating any immediate danger from the weather. A clear sky with high cloud will indicate a clear and sunny day. Dark sky with low cloud normally indicates rain. It is simply a matter of gauging the degree between the two. I do this by looking towards my direction of travel and try to estimate the height of cloud, colour of sky and wind direction. With a little practice one is able to anticipate the weather conditions for several hours ahead.

Winter Hillwalking

The *Gem Hillwalker's Survival Guide* is not intended as a guide to alpine walking. However, it would be unwise not to include details of the basic winter walking techniques.

A covering of snow transforms a landscape of mountains, valleys, streams and trees into a marvellous white blanket. Many walkers like the idea of breaking new ground as they walk through a winter landscape, and take great pleasure from the feeling of isolation this gives. However, winter walking also brings with it many dangers which are not present at other times of the year, and a walker should be appropriately prepared.

FITNESS

Winter walking means trudging through sometimes very deep snow for many hours. The effort required and the energy consumed can be up to three times that for normal walking. Extra clothing, food and fuel will have to be carried, thus increasing the weight of your rucksack, and walking into strong winds or snow blizzards will severely reduce the body's ability to function efficiently. All these extra factors mean that a walker should have a very high level of fitness before venturing out in the winter.

PRECAUTIONS

Walking in the mountains, especially in the Scottish Highlands, during winter is a serious business, and one that should be undertaken only by a group of suitably equipped experienced walkers, preferably with a local guide. All precautions should be taken to balance the walkers' requirement for a sense of freedom with the risk to the lives of those who may have to search for and rescue them.

Make sure that you go out properly equipped against the harshest of elements, and that you carry sufficient survival equipment to see you through any emergency. A sensible walker will carefully consider and plan his route across the winter terrain in advance, making sure that the walk can be completed in daylight (a maximum of six hours and often shorter in the Scottish Highlands), leaving a plan of his route with a responsible person. Ridge walking should be avoided whenever possible, especially where cornices of overhanging snow have formed. Under no circumstances should you venture close to edge of a cornice as from above it will be unclear where the rock ends and the overhang begins. Steep-sided mountains may well harbour areas of snow-covered scree, and while the surface may look intact, underlying rock may well slide away.

AVALANCHES

It is almost impossible to predict when an avalanche is going to occur. Even in Europe, where scientists have studied the phenomenon for years, it is still difficult to forecast a precise time and place. However, slopes which have an angle of between 30° and 45°, and where the depth of snow is more than 30 cm (1 ft), are those which are most at risk from avalanches. It is therefore important to recognize the factors which cause avalanches.

The ground may have been previously covered with a layer of old snow which has deteriorated through fluctuations in temperature to form a smooth, hard, flat surface. A thicker layer of soft snow may well have built up on top of this base. The angle of slope, gravity and the speed and direction of the wind will all contribute to making the top layer of snow move, thus causing an avalanche. This sort of avalanche is know as a soft slab avalanche and is the most common type.

AVALANCHE ASSESSMENT

Knowledge of snowfalls in the previous week, the temperature and the wind strength will all help in an assessment of what lies beneath any fresh snow fall. Asking local guides about high-risk areas and adjusting your route accordingly is also a good idea. Continue to adjust your assessment during your walk, by taking note of how the snow is reacting to your weight on it – is the snow crisp and firm beneath your feet or is it loose and rolling away down the slope? If you see snow breaking up and falling away, even in a small area, you should consider yourself at risk and move if at all possible to level ground.

USING AN ICE AXE

If you are walking during the winter, the chances are that at some point you will have to climb a steep snow-covered slope. An ice axe is therefore an advisable item of equipment to carry. This is a mountaineering tool which has a blade-shaped adze and a curved serrated pick attached to a spiked shaft. Ice axes come in a variety of lengths, but for hillwalking an axe with a handle 70 cm (2 ft) long is recommended. A sling should also be attached to the axe so that it can be put round the wrist and not lost in the event of a fall.

On flat ground an ice axe is best carried attached to the outside of your rucksack or in a holster around the waist. Only when climbing, traversing or descending should the ice axe be used. When in use, the ice axe should be held in the right hand, gripping the head where it meets the shaft, as one would a walking stick

When walking uphill, the shaft is best pushed into the snow for support, while you make steps in the snow with your boots. On steeper slopes or while traversing, you may find it easier to use a two-handed grip on the axe.

When descending a steep slope, it is best to face inwards towards the slope, using both hands on the ice axe for support, and making steps with the toes of your boots. On gently-sloping downhill slopes, it is safe to walk forwards, using the axe as a walking stick and by digging in the heels of your boots for support.

If you should fall on a snow-covered slope, you should use your ice axe to break your slide. There are a number of methods for arresting your fall by using an ice axe, but the following method is safe to use in most situations.

If you feel yourself falling, always try to sit down in the snow, gripping the ice axe head in your left hand and with your right hand firmly on the shaft about half way down. As you start to slide, dig the point of the shaft into the snow as hard as you can, and hold it there. You may not stop straight away, but the action will certainly arrest your fall. At the first opportunity, roll off your back and face the snow, at the same time driving the pick head into the snow with as much force as possible. This action should stop your fall.

AUTHOR'S NOTE

Ice axes are dangerous tools, and unless they are properly used can cause injury. During a fall, always try to keep your ice axe under control. It is highly recommended that you take instruction in the use of an ice axe if you intend to use it for anything more than hillwalking.

Checklist for Winter Walking

- Check the weather forecast before setting off (see page 164).

- Consult a local guide or expert about the route you intend to follow.
- Plan your route with care and leave a copy of it with a responsible person.
- Have a cut-off time for your return.
- Do not walk alone.
- Dress using the layer principle (see page 45). Salopettes are warmer than trousers for winter walking. You should protect your hands and head with thermal gloves, a neck-over and a balaclava.
- Wear comfortable walking boots which are appropriate for winter use.
- Wear gaiters to protect your boots and lower legs.
- Carry an ice axe, but learn how to use it beforehand (see page 169).
- The amount of calories in the food you carry should be twice that for a summer walk.
- Remember to carry a flask of hot soup, as portable cookers do not work well in wintry conditions.
- Watch where you walk. Keep a lookout for signs of avalanches (see page 167).
- Keep a careful watch on the weather.
- If you get into trouble, retrace your steps or walk towards the nearest point of known safety.

Search and Rescue

Hillwalking is not a dangerous pastime, but certain areas in Britain can be quite isolated, and while in the normal course of events this adds to the attraction, it also adds to the risk. Unfortunately, if you are injured or become immobilized, or get caught in unexpected rough weather, this isolation can hamper attempts to locate and rescue you. Luckily, Britain has one of the best search and rescue organizations in the world, and given that you, as a hillwalker, stick to some basic procedures, the time in which help will arrive can be drastically cut.

If an accident does happen, the most important thing is to keep a cool head and not be panicked into a decision which could deteriorate the situation even further. If you are in a party, the leader should keep calm and keep the rest of the party calm and under control too. First, assess the situation and check for any danger to yourself or others before approaching the casualty. If the casualty has fallen, be very careful about approaching from above as this may cause rocks to be dislodged on top of him.

INJURY

Once the casualty has been reached, make a quick but thorough check for any injuries or conditions that may be life-threatening (see page 134). Assess if there are further dangers in the immediate area, either to the casualty, yourself or other members of the party. If so, are you able to move the patient without further injury? At all costs avoid unnecessary treatments or moving the patient when there is any danger of spinal injury, as this could have disastrous consequences. It is important to keep the patient as comfortable and as warm as possible, so if shelter and a source of warmth are available, make use of them, ensuring that the casualty is well insulated.

Quickly assess if the situation is life-threatening or not. High blood-loss or acute respiratory failure will require prompt removal of the casualty to hospital if he is to survive. If the injury is serious, such as a spinal injury, specialized medical assistance will be required before the casualty can be moved. In these cases, outside help in the form of a mountain rescue team will be needed.

LOST

In the short term, simply getting lost does not pose a major problem. If you realize that you have made a map-reading error and aren't where you wanted to be, then you aren't technically lost – just misplaced! Try to work out your position on the map and adjust your route accordingly. If it is not possible to do this but you can see where you want to go, you should proceed. This may well involve retracing your steps or going downhill, but not necessarily. If this is not possible, due to fog, mist or lack of daylight, consider finding a camp site and erecting your tent, or finding an emergency shelter (see page 90). It is up to the individual or party leader to make a decision as to whether to move on or stay put, based on the weather conditions and the terrain.

Being lost for any length of time is normally due to prevailing weather conditions, which not only hamper you and your party, but also any rescue operation. Providing you are not injured, and there are no casualties in your group, the main concern will be protection against hypothermia (see page 150).

FEAR

Fear is an entirely normal, and sometimes necessary, emotion. It is the instinctive reaction of anyone faced with the uncertain, especially when this is a threat to life. Behaviour and reaction are always influenced by fear, and, through them, so are the prospects for survival. Fear can make people do silly things and you could end up with more casualties. It is no good trying to hide from the situation; if you try to cover up in a party of people, it will create an atmosphere of distrust. It is always best to let everyone know the real situation in a calm, optimistic and confident manner. Keep them involved and busy at all levels, from planning the course of action to helping any casualties. Idleness will only give time to reflect on any fears or discomfort.

Acceptance of fear as a natural reaction to any threatening situation will produce two immediate and positive benefits:

- You will be able to dismiss the fear of being afraid, which is often a burden in itself. True courage may be found in people who freely admit to fear, and then go on to do their best in the circumstances they face.

- You will find yourself more likely to be able to carry out considered rather than uncoordinated actions. You will recognize that there is always something that can be done to improve the situation – **never give up hope**.

SHELTER AND SURVIVAL

When forced to stay put either through injury, being lost or being caught out in extreme weather conditions, you should erect your tent or seek some form of shelter if you are to avoid exposure. Tents are by far the quickest and best form of protection, but survival shelters need not be complicated, or take too much time or energy to construct (see page 90). In the most basic terms, you could construct a windbreak from roots or branches, shelter beneath trees and dig a snow trench if appropriate, or wrap yourself in a sleeping bag or spare blanket. You should, if possible, choose your camp site or create your shelter well before dark. Always check the location thoroughly to make sure that it isn't in a place liable to flooding, that there is no danger of a rock fall and that there are no overhanging trees that might fall in a high wind. Keep your shelter small, as this will make it cosy. If you plan to light a fire inside, ensure that you have sufficient ventilation to avoid carbon monoxide poisoning. Always insulate the ground below your body. Sleeping on the earth will quickly rob you of heat.

SURVIVAL KIT

If you are forced to constuct some form of shelter your personal survival pack will be of the utmost importance. It should be carried at all times when the potential for a survival situation exists. Survival kits can be purchased

ready-made and are designed to suit various activities and environments. You may well feel you need to build your own survival kit based on your own experiences and needs. Your decision on the items to be included should be made purely on each item's usefulness, and its adaptability in relation to your type of hillwalking activities. This assessment should be made keeping in mind the strong possibility that the survival kit may be

your only initial resource. However, any survival item
acts as a catalyst for prompting action and calming fear.

Listed below are a selection of possible components for a
personal survival kit, together with notes on their uses.
The items mentioned are those which I strongly
recommend for inclusion. You may find others which are
useful in a particular situation.

- **Matches.** A dozen or more kitchen matches, which
  have been completely immersed in melted candle
  wax, will be both waterproof and wind-resistant.
  They should be carried in a waterproof container.

- **Candle.** A 10 cm (4 in) candle weighs less than 25 g
  (1 oz) yet will burn for up to three hours if it is
  protected from the wind (see page 109).

- **Compass.** A compass is a priority item for your kit.
  A button compass is the ideal choice. It is easy to
  read but takes up the minimum amount of space.

- **Needle.** A needle with a large eye, about 5 cm (2 in)
  long (e.g. Chenille No. 16 or a sail-maker's needle),
  can be used for heavy -duty sewing of materials such
  as shoe leather, rawhide or heavy clothing. It can
  also be magnetized for use as a pointer in an
  improvised compass.

- **Survival bag.** One of the most frequent dangers to
  be faced in a survival situation is the involuntary loss
  of critical amounts of body-heat. This loss occurs
  through convection, conduction or radiation. A
  survival bag is therefore a must (see page 98).

- **Water purification tablets.** These provide a quick and convenient way of sterilizing water. Each tablet will purify 1 litre (2 pints) of water in about ten minutes.

- **Knife.** A Swiss Army-type knife, incorporating a wide variety of functions, is best. It can include extra blades, scissors, can and bottle openers, screwdriver and saw among its many implements. It is strongly recommended that a small pocket knife is carried when hillwalking as a matter of course.

- **Parachute cord.** Many a farmer will tell you that he never goes out without a quantity of string in his pocket. The same principle should apply to hillwalkers, except you would be better off using a 15 m (45 ft) length of parachute cord.

- **Flares.** In a survival situation, signal flares attract attention better than most other methods.

GOING FOR HELP

If you have a problem and need help, visually check the area for other walking or climbing groups nearby. If none is contactable and the party is equipped with a mobile phone, this should be used (if reception is clear) to get in touch with the rescue services. However, you may well have to send members of the party for help. If you do decide to send others, send at least two. These people must be fit, reliable and know exactly what is expected of them. Do not expect them to commit all the relevant knowledge to memory but instead write it on a note to carry with them. There should be enough daylight hours in order for them to reach the nearest rescue post. You should also instruct them on the best route of how to get there or the nearest place from which the rescue services can be contacted. The messengers should be aware that the rescue depends on their getting through safely and that speed is not as important as their safety. The note should contain:

- Your location, with a six-figure grid reference (see page 64).
- The type of terrain you are in, with details of the best approach route.
- Relevant details of any injured party.
- A summary of your plan of action so far.
- The type of help required. If their point of first contact is a telephone, they must use this to contact the rescue services, police, etc.

ALONE

If you are alone, conscious and your injuries do not prevent you from walking, then you should evaluate your situation carefully before moving. This evaluation will be based on that for a group. If no one near you can be contacted, you should balance the dangers and the value of attempting to seek help with those of staying put and letting the rescue services find you.

If you are immobile and unable to walk, the decision will be made for you. In this event you should do all within your capabilities to protect yourself from the elements and prepare some form of signal device with which to attract attention. If you have a tent but are unable to erect it, try folding it around your body. If, due to your injuries, you can only achieve the prone position, do all that is possible to insulate yourself from the ground. In bad visibility, the odds are that any rescue party will be on foot, so blow a whistle at frequent intervals.

Sometimes it is necessary to leave casualties on their own while help is summoned, but this must be considered only as a last resort. An unconscious casualty should never be left alone as his condition may deteriorate very quickly, and without the rendering of immediate first aid he may die. In any case where a casualty is left alone, all possible measures must be taken to ensure his comfort, health and safety. The casualty should be given strict instructions not to move, as this will hamper any rescue attempt. Make sure some form of signal device is left with the casualty, and that you mark the area with something brightly coloured fixed firmly to the ground.

If it happens that the group leader is injured, and left alone, he must ensure before sending others to fetch help that they speak to the relevant people, preferably the leader of the rescue team, or dial 999. They then must ensure that all relevant information is clearly and accurately given when requested, and that any requests from the rescue team are obeyed.

MOUNTAIN RESCUE TEAMS

Mountain rescue teams, of which there are about a hundred in the British Isles, are well-organized and -equipped. They work in collaboration with the RAF and the police in search and rescue operations and training. Local mountain rescue teams also run and maintain mountain rescue posts, identified by an MR sign. It is from these bases that a rescue is normally mounted, although this is not always the case. Some posts, due to their remote nature, are unmanned, but still carry most of the equipment and supplies to enable a rescue attempt to be made.

SEARCH PATTERNS

When searching for a missing individual or party, the rescue services will react to whatever information is available. If the location of an accident is known, a small advance party will be sent out first. These reconnaissance units will consist of three or four very experienced members, who will have an excellent working knowledge of the area. In addition, helicopters and search dogs, should they be required, can be called upon. Advance parties are often lightly equipped, carrying just basic first aid, shelter kits, food and radios. They follow the last-known route of the lost party or will search in any likely places of refuge. Once the casualty has been found, they will provide immediate care, and organize a stretcher party if a helicopter is not available.

If the location is not known, the search and rescue (SAR) services will separate into small mobile teams. The area covered will be based on the best estimated overall guide of the missing person's last-known location. How the search is carried out will be determined by the size of the area to be covered, the terrain, the weather and operational necessity.

If you have followed the correct procedures and notified others of your intended route, or you can establish radio or telephone communication, a contact search will be initiated. This is designed to concentrate rescue efforts on a relatively small area, thus increasing the speed at which rescuers can get to you.

Unless there is accurate knowledge of the location of the party to be rescued, it would be futile and even risky to send a search team out at night. However, certain refuge points, such as mountain huts and bothies, will sometimes be checked. At times, when there is no known route or precise location, the mountain rescue teams may establish a forward base where stretchers and heavier equipment can be left, while searches continue using one of the following main methods:

- **Area search.** This involves dividing up the area into smaller sections using natural features as landmarks. These provide boundaries within which individual teams can search.

- **Sweep search.** The rescue party spreads out in a line and searches the area in a disciplined and organized manner.

- **Contact search.** A search focussed on a smaller area but based on the principles of the sweep search.

- **Dog search.** The advantage of search dogs is that they work using their sense of smell rather than sight, and are capable of tracking ground scent for up to forty-eight hours, and even longer in ideal conditions. If required, search dogs can work as well in the dark as they can in the light.

HELICOPTER MOUNTAIN RESCUE OPERATIONS

As mentioned earlier, mountain rescue teams in Britain are highly skilled and have access to excellent resources, including RAF helicopters and front-line medical care. However, it would be a dangerous mistake to assume that they will always be there to get you out of danger. For various reasons, such as the rescue team not knowing your location or serious weather conditions, the team may not always be able to get to you in time. Therefore, it is always better to have a good degree of self-reliance, so that your chances of survival in an emergency will be increased. If you set out with an attitude of independence and competence, then not only will you be able to help yourself in an emergency, but you will also be able to aid others in distress.

With forethought and the correct equipment and skills, the experienced individual or leader of a party should be able to deal with most emergency situations that arise. However, even with the best planning and the most experienced people, accidents can still happen, and even a minor injury or incident, when it happens in the mountains, can often become something far worse if the correct procedures are not followed.

The team leader should be aware that a helicopter will take some time to carry out a rescue, as strict safety procedures must be adhered too. Helicopter crews can take a considerable amount of time assessing the possible problems that may be encountered in a mountainous rescue site. It is not uncommon on very windy days for a pilot to have several attempts at establishing a hover close enough to the casualty to be able to get a winch man or mountain rescue team to their position. Having

arrived at a workable hover, the next priority is to assess
the safest method of rescuing the casualty. To ensure no
important aspect of the situation is overlooked, RAF
crews use a standardized system of assessment and
briefing.

The following priorities normally govern the decision-
making process:

- Aircraft safety
- Winch man safety
- Survivor safety

It may seem odd to place the casualty at the bottom of
the priority list, but there is little justification for
endangering the lives of several rescuers unless the
situation demands it. Rescue attempts are, therefore, all
about risk assessment.

SIGNALLING

One of the first priorities in any survival situation is
communication. If at all possible, the survivor must let
the outside world know that he needs help.

Check whatever means of communication is available to
you. If you have a mobile phone which is receiving a
signal, it could place you in direct communication with a
helicopter winchman. (I am reliably informed that most
RAF winchmen carry a mobile phone during any rescue
operation. If you are carrying a mobile phone, make sure
its presence is relayed in your request for the emergency
services.)

A Locaid radar reflective balloon is extremely useful when on excursions into remote areas

RADAR BALLOON

There are several radar reflective balloons on the market, some of which fly like a kite, while others are gas-filled. The best of these is the Locaid, which is quick and easy to operate, and will fly in all types of weather, including strong winds. The Locaid is hand-held in a similar way to a pyrotechnic flare. The safety tape is removed, allowing the balloon to be operated by the removal of a safety pin. The balloon inflates automatically in an aerodynamic shape, and then lifts off to fly at around 35 m (105 ft), where it is tethered by a line to the hand mechanism. The foil reflective balloon can be seen over 38 km (24 miles) away and the Locaid will stay aloft for up to five days.

VISUAL AND SOUND SIGNALS

These are perhaps the easiest signals to create, mainly using basic items from a survival kit. They can work well over long distances and, in some cases, when visibility is severely restricted.

FIRE

One of the best signal-producers is fire. A fire should be prepared and kept ready for lighting at the first sign of help arriving. For daytime use it is best to produce a high smoke volume by adding green vegetation to an established fire. At night, a bright clear flame is required. This can be achieved by burning old, dry fuel.

HELIOGRAPH

Using the sun's reflection is an excellent way of signalling for help. If you do not possess a heliograph, any mirrored surface, i.e. a vanity mirror, a wristwatch or a piece of glass, will work.

TORCH

At night even a small torch can be seen from a great distance in the right weather conditions. Remember to conserve your batteries for just such an event. If you have no torch, consider using the flash on a camera.

FLARES

Small packs of survival flares can be purchased from most leading camping stores or chandlers. Care should be exercised with their use as they are a potential weapon. Always follow the instructions to the letter and aim the flare skywards. Any flare pistol should only be operated by a fully competent person. Once fired, the flare will reach a height of around 100 m (300 ft) and should be visible for many miles, depending on the weather conditions. Normally a red flare means help, but firing any flare in the mountains will attract attention.

WHISTLE

Almost every survival kit will contain a whistle and this is one device that you can use to your heart's content. Recent innovations have produced a new kind of whistle, which produces a very high pitch. Its range is claimed to be over 1000 m (3000 ft). Give six quick blasts one after the other, repeated after one minute.

GROUND SIGNALS

The letters and configurations shown on the opposite page are used in ground-to-air recognition signals. When constructing them take into account that a pilot may be a long way off and therefore the size and background colour contrast of the signal is extremely important. This can be done by making your signals at least 5 m (15 ft) long and about 1.5 m (5 ft) wide. Black earth against light-coloured grass, or shadow created by tramping down fresh snow or laying down fir branches, will all add to the contrast.

I Require a doctor and Casevac

II Need medical supplies

F Need food and water

N/A No and Yes (i.e. affirmative)

LL Everything OK

X Unable to move

→ Moving this way

☐ Need compass and map

▲ Safe to land

WHEN HELP ARRIVES

Make yourself as obvious as possible. A Day-Glo panel, such as an orange survival bag, can easily be seen from the air. At night, flash a torch, but as the helicopter approaches direct the beam at the ground. This is because the crew may be using night vision goggles to improve safety, and even small external light sources shone directly at them can seriously reduce the goggles' efficiency or stop them working altogether. All search and rescue helicopters are fitted with powerful floodlighting.

Remember that a helicopter will approach a selected landing site into the wind, so stand well to the windward side of the aircraft. If you know where the helicopter is going to land, or have marked out a landing site yourself, make sure that it is as clear as possible of debris and that you have firmed any dry snow by stamping it down. Do not rush at the helicopter as it lands, but wait for a signal from the pilot or winch man indicating that it is safe to do so. Secure any loose equipment before the helicopter arrives in the hover and expect some downwash from the rotor blades. If the pick-up site is very steep or dangerous and requires a winch man to be lowered, try to prepare a belay (a firm anchor point to which something can be attached) for the winch man's use on his arrival. Carry out the winch man's instructions to the letter.

Useful Addresses

British Mountaineering
Council Information
Service
177-179 Burton Road
Manchester
M20 2BB

Mountaineering Council
of Scotland
4a St Catherine's Road
Perth
PH1 5SE

American Hiking Society
PO Box 20160
Washington DC

Long Distance Walkers
Association
c/o Les Maple
21 Upcroft
Windsor
Berkshire
SL4 3NH

Mountain Bothies
Association
26 Rycroft Avenue
Deeping St James
Peterborough
PE6 8NT

The National Trust
36 Queen Anne's Gate
London
SW1H 9AS

The National Trust for
Scotland
5 Charlotte Square
Edinburgh
EH2 4DU

Plas-y-Brenin National
Mountain Centre
Capel Curig
Conwy
LL24 0ET

Glenmore Lodge
Aviemore
Inverness
PH22 1QU

National Outdoor
Leadership School
Dept R
288 Main Street
Lander WY 82520

Outward Bound
Route 90
R2, Box 280
Garrison NY 10524

The Ramblers'
Association
1-5 Wandworth Road
London
SW8 2XX

Ulster Federation of
Rambling Clubs
c/o Mary Doyle
27 Slievegallion Drive
Belfast
BT11 8JN

The British Red Cross
Society
9 Grosvenor Crescent
London
SW1X 7EJ

St John's Ambulance
1 Grosvenor Crescent
London
SW1X 7EF

St Andrews Ambulance
Association
St Andrews House
Milton Street
Glasgow
G4 0HR

American Red Cross
National Headquarters
431 18th Street NW
Washington DC 20006

Youth Hostels
Association
Trevelyan House
8 St Stephen's Hill
St Albans
Herts
AL1 2DY

Scottish Youth Hostels
Association
7 Glebe Crescent
Stirling
FK8 2JA

Youth Hostels
Association of Northern
Ireland
22 Donegall Road
Belfast
BT12 5JN

Hostelling International-
American Youth Hostels
733 15th Street NW
840
Washington DC 20005